THE MERCURY MAN

Freddie Mercury In My Life

Mary Howis

APEX

First published in 2004, reprinted and updated in 2009
This edition published in 2015 by
Apex Publishing Ltd
12A St. John's Road, Clacton on Sea
Essex, CO15 4BP, United Kingdom
www.apexpublishing.co.uk

Typesetting and layout by
Andrews UK Limited
www.andrewsuk.com

Preface

This is a story about Freddie Mercury, lead singer of the rock band Queen, known in the spirit world as 'the Mercury Man'.

It isn't a story of his life on Earth as such, it's mainly about life since he passed into the spirit world.

Freddie Mercury (or precisely the spirit who chose to become Freddie Mercury on his last visit to Earth) has been travelling along by my side spiritually since the day after he passed from the Earth.

This will not make sense to a lot of the people who read this book, because I do realize this concept is very hard to take in, even for me. But as the story progresses it will, I am sure, make more sense to you. Hopefully, it will be fascinating and full of love to such people who understand these things. It isn't really written for the true Freddie Mercury fans, although I am sure that the fact that you all loved him so much when he was on Earth will make you intrigued and, for those of you who are spiritually minded, also very glad for him, knowing that his life still goes on, and didn't just come to an end on that awful November day in 1991 when you all took it for granted that you had lost him.

But if you believe in the spirit world, which I do very strongly basically because of the FREDDIE MERCURY EXPERIENCE, I hope it helps you believe even stronger. And if you don't believe in the spirit world and you are just reading this book out of curiosity, I hope it opens up something inside you to help you find that belief. Because if you could just find it, it helps us to see our lives and Freddie's that touch some of us in a different way.

I have had many, many experiences and received information for myself from Freddie Mercury. Information has also been passed on to me from him via different mediums, especially one good friend who is an extremely gifted medium, who has sat patiently with me for many an hour and connected up to the spirit world for me to help to get this information through, to help to put this book together. He wishes to remain unnamed, and just did it to help me and out of his great love of the spirit world and how it has changed and enhanced his life over the years and has given him a chance to help others. But

I thank him deeply, for without him I would be lost and this book, I am sure, would never have been written.

He was not the only bully that I have met in my life who confused the meaning of respect with fear. In 1987, I arrived in Basildon, Essex after being released from a prison sentence for wounding. There, I began work at a nightclub called Raquel's where the clientele appeared to be only interested in either fucking or fighting one other. My fellow doormen were at best inadequate with dealing with the battles that raged each night. They were local men who `respected` the local bullies who had earned their reputation in the playground and who were determined to take them to their graves. It was my view, that the sooner that happened the better.

After confronting the head of security about his spineless attitude, he walked out of the club and I took over. Within weeks I had brought in a man named Tony Tucker as my partner. Tucker controlled a large and extremely `influential` door firm that was 'respected' throughout London and Essex. At first things went well. We cleared Raquel's of the local bullies (usually head first via the three storey concrete stair case) and decent people once more began to frequent the premises. In the early 1990`s the love drug Ecstasy arrived in club land and Tucker and I found ourselves in a position to control a very lucrative market. Dealers would pay rent to sell drugs in the club and soon we were enjoying a lifestyle that neither of us had ever before experienced. However, the more money we earned, the more concerned I became. I could see beyond the smiling faces that showed Tucker and I `respect` and who wanted to be our `friends.` Meaningless, empty people who wanted a piece of the action to enrich their miserable lives would do their best to immerse themselves in the murky world that we inhabited. I chose to avoid them, Tucker chose to exploit them. He would ply young men with bags of pills and packets of powder. They would then be dispatched to various clubs throughout London and Essex to earn him money. Inevitably some dealers would take the drugs themselves, give them to friends or occasionally get caught in possession by the police. Regardless of their sob story, Tucker would always want his money. If the dealers were unable to pay, Tucker would take great pleasure in subjecting them to cruel and merciless violence. `If I let one off, they will all take the piss, they have to respect me,` he would say. In December 1995, Tucker and two of his associates went to meet one of the dealers that had failed to pay his dues. The dealer, a rather nondescript individual who has never been known to be violent before, had already suffered the wrath of Tony Tucker previously, but he had decided that he wasn't going to suffer it any more. He wasn't angry, he was in fact scared, but the beast that resides within us all had been unleashed. He knew what he had to do, the bully who confused respect with fear had to die. When the Range Rover carrying Tucker and his associates pulled up at a Farmer's gate that night, the middle aged drug dealer approached the car. In his hand he grasped a Spas.12 semiautomatic pump action shotgun. Moments later, Tucker and his associates were dead but the gunman continued to fire into their motionless heads. All of the fear, the anger and the hatred that he had felt for Tucker was finally being expelled. As three men had died, a new man had been born; one who knew the true meaning of respect. Never would he confuse fear with respect because he had endured it. The man had learned that you cannot respect anybody until you respect yourself. To have self respect you have principles, stand up for yourself and treat others as you would wish to be treated. To have self respect you have to love and cherish those closest to you. To have self respect you have to honour the wishes of others. And if you do these things, you don't have to think about giving others respect or earning it, because you will have already done both.

THE MERCURY MAN

Chapter 1

Most of us know that Freddie Mercury passed away on 24 November 1991; how could we not know. He was one of the biggest rock superstars the world has known and what a loss it was. Such a young life snuffed out just like that with so much talent still packed inside him, so much that we would never know about now. The fans were devastated across the world; everybody knew and loved Freddie Mercury it seems. Except for me, who didn't even know who this man was. I first heard that he had died the day after his death, on the evening news. I listened more carefully as he was obviously someone very well known because of the coverage given. I became completely overwhelmed with sadness as though I had lost my very best friend, but there was no sensible reason for this, because I had nothing to relate to. This is where my strange journey with Freddie started all those years ago.

I don't want this story to be a whimsical fantasy-type story that seems to be mocking Freddie Mercury's memory. I want it to be as factual as possible; something that you can maybe understand and see some sense in; something you may be able to relate to, that has happened in your own lives, but you are perhaps afraid to mention for fear of being ridiculed. I myself have had to summon up a lot of courage to get this book together, but if this is what I am required to do then I will do it for him and take my chances.

I would just like to add that the sole aim of this book is to prove without a shadow of a doubt that life goes on after we seemingly die and leave this Earth. Freddie Mercury feels that if through him this can be proved it will fulfil all the things he didn't get to achieve through his life on Earth.

Chapter 2

Inevitably this story is also about myself since Freddie came into my life and intermingled with mine; otherwise it would make no sense.

How did I feel in the first stages of this experience of mine? My first sense, as I can remember was a great sadness around me, but also from the very beginning I felt a kind of presence around me. It's hard to describe what that means; it's like there is something, somebody, there with you, something you can't see, yet is almost like a comfort to you. It has been a long time now and I have only come to understand this myself as time has gone on and I can look back at it all.

I was at a fairly low ebb in my life when Freddie passed away, so I wondered whether this was the reason that I felt this way; was it something to latch on to and cling to? However, I knew deep down in my soul somehow this wasn't the reason. But there had to be some logical explanation. He was always there in my mind, this unknown person. It was like an obsession growing. I started buying lots of Queen music, any books that were around giving me information about him. But all through this, although I enjoyed a lot of the songs and only half-heartedly read the books, there was always something about this man pulling at my heartstrings; and every morning when I opened my eyes there was the image of this man imprinted on my mind. (When I look back now after all these years I realize that he was trying to get my attention, to let me know that he had survived somehow, but I didn't understand these things enough then.)

Then odd things started happening. It turned out that my friend Joan really liked Queen music, although prior to this I had never heard her mention Queen and we had been friends for a long time. But anyway she said she'd come over to my house and we could listen to the music together. While we were sitting there, a mist appeared on the stairs and slowly started to move along and descend them. (We both saw it clearly.) Then it floated across in front of us never stopping, just slowly moving on. There is a mirror over the fireplace in the front room and we distinctly saw this misty stuff as it slowly passed in front of it. Reflected in the mirror it drifted past and on through the dining room and then disappeared. We were both absolutely amazed. We didn't have a clue what it was but I do remember Joan saying, "My God, I think you have got Freddie Mercury here". Neither of us had ever experienced anything like this before in our lives. Of course we both laughed and didn't take what she said seriously; it was just something neither of us understood and was strange to us.

The image in my mind's eye of Freddie has always been the same, right from the very beginning of all this to the present. I see him with short hair, a moustache and wearing a white vest. I have obviously over the years seen many different pictures of him at many different stages in his life but my own personal image of him never falters from this one face.

One night soon after the experience with the mist, I had a vivid dream. I was standing in a room quite high up somewhere, looking out through a large window that covered the whole of one wall. The view was absolutely beautiful: an area of water, very calm water, and trees in the background. I remember thinking this is so calming and a wonderful feeling, I could stay like this forever. Then I felt someone by me, who put their arm around my waist. I looked and it was Freddie Mercury, just as solid as me, and he said, "Now that I have shown you this you must go back my dear", and kissed me on the cheek.

This is years ago now but it is still as vivid as if it was last night and is an experience I have always treasured. I still don't know what he was showing me. Peace, was he just showing me what peace within yourself was like; was he showing me a memory of his that he treasured and wanted to share with me? I don't know, but I do know that now the years have progressed and things have come together and with all the information that I have gained over the years, the dream was a true experience that it was him making himself known to me.

By now a lot of you must be asking yourselves: if this person was experiencing the presence of Freddie Mercury why did he choose her? She didn't even know who he was before he died. She had no interest in his life. Why didn't he pick a fan? Well, I don't know either. That has been the hardest part of experiencing all this. But I have been told through a medium, as time has gone on, that he found me more than chose me. But it was better that I wasn't a fan because my mind would be clearer, more open to what he wanted.

There is one thing I need to say before I continue: this story isn't just for my benefit, it's for all of you to gain something from. I have just been fortunate enough for it to be able to come through me.

I would say that for the first fifteen months of this experience, except for a few other odd things happening such as feeling arms around me when I was feeling a bit low, which somehow made me feel better instead of frightened, it was basically like an obsession about this man. He always seemed to be in my mind, but it did make up for other empty things in my life. So I would say, yes, I enjoyed it. It gave me comfort, something to focus on, but then there seemed to be a different, stronger presence around me. Like someone or something was forcefully trying to get my attention to the extent that it felt as though someone had got their hands on my back, pushing me along, trying so hard to be noticed and to get me to find out more about what was happening. I had throughout this time discussed this situation of mine with my friend Joan. She suggested that perhaps we should go to a Spiritualist Church. I didn't like the idea but thought, well, it can't do any harm. It will be a new experience in my life, seeing how these mediums work.

So I and my friend ventured off to a Spiritualist Church, I didn't expect to experience anything more than watching how these mediums are able to pass on messages to families who have lost their loved ones. I didn't expect anything for myself because the experience I was having was (if there was any truth in it) coming from a stranger to me. So how could anything be told to me? We sat at the back of the church, hoping we wouldn't be noticed, and then we could clear off easily at the end. But through the course of this evening I had a shock, because I had a message. The medium that evening was a man called Bruce James. I had never seen this person before this night, but he gave me a message, saying there was a gentleman who had passed into the spirit world who had connected up with me when he left this world. The medium wasn't willing to give the message giver's name but he knew I was aware of him because he had been around me for quite a while now. The medium said the message the gentleman was sending was that he knew I was at a bit of a low ebb and he wanted me to be a bit happier, and a bit more flamboyant in my life. I remember thinking, that's strange; I've heard it said that Freddie Mercury was thought of as flamboyant what a strange message. At the end of the evening, Bruce James came over to Joan and me and said he could see that we hadn't been to a Spiritualist Church before, and asked if we would like to go to his home one evening so that he could explain things better to us. So we accepted his invitation and went to see him and his wife the following week.

When we had settled down, he said to me, "I must tell you this, I have seen you twice now, and each time you have had a gentleman from the spirit world walking beside you". He continued, "He is quite tall, about 5ft 8ins, slim, with short black hair and a moustache, and he says he died when he was 45 and he is asking me to tell you that now he has found you he will always stay with you". This shocked me so greatly that everyone must have seen it on my face. Bruce was very apologetic about this, and said, "Oh dear, have you lost your husband recently?" I said no, but I did feel there had been someone (or something) around me for a while. Bruce then told me that this gentleman had something else to say to me. This was that one day I would meet someone who he had considered as part of his close family. When I met this person I must promise him that I would pass on a very important message for him. So I agreed half-hearted and remembered being completely bewildered with it all. This was seventeen months after Freddie had died. I saw Bruce quite often for a while after this, but he never knew who this person (spirit) with me was and I never told him. I held inside me the message for this person I would supposedly meet, never thinking for one second the day would come that I would meet this person. I took it for granted really that if it the message was for anyone, it must be Freddie Mercury's parents, and I certainly wouldn't be making a fool of myself and telling them anything.

Naturally, by this time I was very intrigued with all of this. Was there really a possibility, after all, that Freddie Mercury, or whatever he was now in spirit form, was connecting up with me somehow? It certainly was beginning to seem likely, but why me? Because of everything I had been told I just had to go back to the Spiritualist Church to see if there was anything else that I could learn, and learn I certainly did. I discovered that none of us actually dies, we all have to go through the process of our earthly death, we can't escape that, however it may happen. But that isn't the end. Our life down on Earth is just a part of something else; something that goes on forever. Of course the body that we live in on Earth doesn't survive.

Each week there were different mediums coming to the church. All new to me, they came from all over the country. It was all new and fascinating.

The next clear message I got was from a medium a gentleman I didn't know at all. But now, all these years later, he is my very good friend and the person who has brought some of the information through to me from Freddie.

What I was told by this person was that the spirit world was feeding information through to him, that a man who had been very well known to the public had died in London, who was in his mid-forties when he passed over and his death had completely changed my life. I remember panicking thinking, my God, he is going to say it's Freddie Mercury to all these people and then they will all laugh and say to one another, who does she think she is, thinking she is so special. So I denied it, and said no I didn't understand this at all. So the medium, my friend of now, got quite irate and said, "Look dear, I only bring the truth through. If you don't want the message I won't waste my time" and moved on to someone else. Of course, then I was annoyed with myself for being such a coward and losing out on what the full message was going to be. When I look back at this, it was so silly of me to react in that way but it was a very hard concept to take on board, that a stranger to me, who died, especially a superstar like Freddie Mercury, had latched on to my life. But this has gone on for twelve years now, and inside myself, within my own thoughts of him, he has been one of my greatest comforts and the most constant friend I have ever known. And now I can quite confidently tell you all that I love him to bits.

By this time it was 1993. The feeling of someone close around me continued and this strong feeling of love surrounding me, although it was invisible, was really nice and comforting, not frightening at all; strange yes, hard to understand yes, but never frightening. I listened to Freddie's music a lot, and many of the words seemed to imprint themselves on my mind, making me wonder whether he was trying to tell us all something even before he died, especially in his latter songs, maybe not even realizing himself. Were some of the words to his songs being related to him from some inner source, one that we all carry without knowing it?

I continued to go along to the Spiritualist Church receiving many messages, but certainly not all the messages were from Freddie. My gran, who had passed away many years before, started coming through with things, telling me she was fine, that it had been a great shock to her that she had survived after her earthly death because she had always believed that when you're dead you're dead and that's the end. But I was learning fast that it obviously isn't; how else were these messages coming through? These people must have survived, or at least their spirits had survived. My gran said she had been longing for me to come to a place where she could get these messages through to me. To let me know that her life had carried on and that she was happy, and was always close beside me. This brought a lot of joy into my life because I was brought up with my mother and grandmother, so she had been a very important part of my life. My memory of her all these previous years, because she passed away in 1973, had been very precious. Now it was almost like having her given back to me, and being able to tell my mother that I had heard from my gran was comforting to her. I was never completely convinced that my mother truly believed it, but I know it did at least make her think about such things.

However, in the end she had no choice, because my mother passed away in September 2001 at the age of ninety, and I have had many wonderful messages back from her. But the main one that will stay with me forever was that my grandmother was waiting for her when she passed over. The actual message was, "I knew I had died because when I opened my eyes my mother was there with me". So because of this Freddie Mercury experience of mine, because this is what was spurring me on, I was learning all sorts of other comforting things. When I was sixteen a boy, a friend of mine, but not a close friend, was killed instantly in a motorbike accident; he was also sixteen, so it was years ago and I had forgotten all about it. But he came through with a message, telling me he was all right and he had survived his earthly death. I explained to the medium that I didn't know him that well so why would he come through to me. She explained that when someone on the other side is desperate to communicate they will quietly watch until someone comes along to a Spiritualist Church or something similar for example, a gathering of spiritually minded people and they will if they can get their message through. She said as long as I accept him and the message he sent through that he is okay that will make him happy. So I did and I have heard from him quite a few times since.

I compiled a couple of tapes of Queen songs to play in the car, some of my now favourites. They were basically just for company when I was driving along on my own. One of them was a song called 'Breakthru', and to this day I have never been able to figure out how this happened, but every time I got back into the car from any destination I had been to and put the tape on the first words that would come through were always the same. How this happened made no sense at all because I wasn't always making the same journey so there was no connection with the time space. It wasn't that the tape just happened to be switched on at the same spot every time and yet it just kept happening for weeks. So I confided very reluctantly in a couple of people from the Spiritualist Church. Having explained the situation to them, they were definitely not as surprised as I expected them to be. They said there was nothing strange about this, and that once you get to know about spirit life a bit more you will see that spirits can control things to draw your attention, not to scare you, just to make themselves known to you. They weren't even surprised it was Freddie Mercury. They said they had heard of this before people who had been famous passing over to the other side and reaching out to someone like me. One example was a lady who had had an experience like this with Marilyn Monroe. I eventually met this lady and she said, yes, she had had Marilyn Monroe close to her for a long time and it had been a shock to her. But she had learned to communicate with her and she had, in the end, enjoyed the experience. She told me that she couldn't feel the experience any more but it had been in her life. This lady I am talking about, I can assure you, is very normal. She suggested that I try to communicate with this spirit, I asked how and when to do that, she told me to find some time for myself each day, somewhere quiet, just sit relaxed, clear my mind of all daily thoughts and simply just say, "Come on Freddie I'll listen to you. I am quite happy for you to draw close to me". The lady then said any thoughts that came into my mind that I knew were not my own to write them down, and see if they made sense with my situation.

So I started to do this and found it quite enjoyable if only for having some quiet, peaceful time to myself. All I could feel around me really though was this same loving presence. I couldn't seem to communicate as this lady had explained. So instead I asked a question. I said, "If this is definitely you around me Freddie, there is talk going around that another Queen album is going to be released, with some new songs contained in it. If you could tell me the title of the very last song you ever wrote and it turns out to be true then that is complete proof to me that this is you". And I instantly heard a voice speaking to me, or someone else's thought running through my mind. This is what I heard: "I can't tell you that dear, because someone along the line will say it was leaked out somehow and will never believe you, but I will tell you this: my last song is filled with "Every day there's a small wonder to be found". Write these words down dear, keep them safe and you will see the sense in this in the end and thank you for drawing close to me and asking me this". Of course after this was over and I thought it all through I really believed I had just got a wild imagination, but I wrote the words down anyway never forgetting them. I even phoned a friend of mine and asked her to write these words down as well and keep them safe.

I must admit I couldn't wait for this next album to be released (just in case). So the day that it was I was outside the shop as soon as it opened. I couldn't wait to get back home to listen to it. I thought maybe one of the lines to a song would be "Every day there's a wonder to be found". But, no, these words didn't exist. So, then as I listened more carefully, disappointed I must admit, I started to take in the words from 'A Winter's Tale'. They sounded very much to me like "Every day there's a small wonder to be found".

One of his songs is so obviously about every day; even if we are having a bad day, there is always a small wonder to be found, and I try to live like that now, because I have bad days like we all do. But now I try to look for one small wonder each day, and it really helps. I don't know if Freddie wrote all the words to this song, or if other Queen members wrote some of them, but however it came together Freddie Mercury certainly knew about it.

I am sure this is the last song he ever wrote. I hope I have got this story right, but it seems he went to Montreux, sat by the lake where his statue is now and wrote this song, then came back to his home in England and passed away a couple of weeks later.

I can't tell you all the things that have happened to me where my Freddie Mercury experiences are concerned. Not because I don't want to, it's just that it would never all fit into this book, and there are other things I want this book to contain. But I will tell you about this one incident. I went to the Spiritualist Church one evening, and there was a lady medium there that evening from another part of the country. She was obviously quite well known and popular, although I had never heard of her. The place was packed, which was unusual, so I sat close to the back completely surrounded by people. You could say lost in the crowd. But, halfway through the messages being communicated, the lady looked straight over to me. She said, "I have got a gentleman in the spirit world here for you and he is saying, look at her hiding away, she thinks I can't see her". She went quiet for a second or two then she asked "Have you got a gentleman in the spirit world who has become a very good friend of yours, but you never knew him on Earth?" I replied, "Yes I believe I have". She continued, "This is very unusual for a thing like this to happen, but not impossible. He is obviously very fond of you, and glad he has found you, but he is saying, tell her for me, will you, that she won't be spending all her life coming to places like this. There are lots of other things I want her to do. Tell her I will stay close to her, and show her the way." The medium lady seemed a bit bewildered with this message because she didn't know who this man was and how he would fit into my life. She was just being told he had connected up with me after he had passed over to the other side. I was beginning to wonder myself. I thought, these messages keep coming through for me so why doesn't he just say this is Freddie Mercury, although I admit I was afraid of this being mentioned in case people ridiculed me. I know I had, by this time, confided in a couple of people about this situation and they seemed fine about it, but that certainly isn't the same as the general public hearing a thing like this. However, I have since learned, way down the line of the story, that celebrities on the other side are just as worried about telling these mediums who they are in case the message doesn't get passed on, because it takes a very brave, confident medium to say they have got someone like this coming through, for fear of their own reputation going down the drain.

Chapter 3

I had joined the Queen fan club by now and shortly after I received this message one of the club magazines arrived. I was gazing through it when I noticed a small advert. It said something like: 'This man who died has changed my life completely'. So my first reaction to this was that someone else must have had the same or similar experience to me. Then it went on to say about looking for people to collect money in a street collection, for the Mercury Phoenix Trust, and it suddenly crossed my mind about poor Freddie dying of AIDS. Oh, of course I knew he had, but I just never gave it any thought, and for some reason it made me feel quite ashamed of myself. So I phoned the lady who had put the advert in the magazine. I told her a bit about my experiences where Freddie was concerned and asked her if she had had similar experiences. She said that she hadn't. It was because she had been a fan of Freddie's and had been very upset when he died. This is what had really spurred her on with the Mercury Phoenix Trust supporting, but she said it was a bit like an unseen force spurring her on, making her very determined to do this thing and achieve the very best results she could. She said it was a shame we lived so far apart because it would be nice to come over and see me, and maybe having a chat with me, in the hope that everything that was happening to her, this thing driving her on, would make more sense. I said I would be happy to help with the street collection for the Trust, so she told me there was a local coordinator who lived not very far away from me and to get in touch with her, which I did. We got on very well together, and it all went from there.

A few of us got together and went with our collection boxes to our local town at the beginning of December 1994. That day really opened my eyes. We did collect quite a lot of money but a couple of people did say to me, "You don't expect us to give money for that do you? They should live a different life". I was getting irate about this, but somehow I managed to carry on smiling. Then a lady came up to me and put a twenty pound note into my collection box. She started to cry and said, "Can't anybody do anything for these poor people?" She continued, "My best friend died of AIDS and it was awful. She gave me a hug and said thank you for caring, and went on her way". So by this time all sorts of thoughts were going through my mind. One of them was, have people still really got an attitude towards AIDS? It just shows how naive I was at that time.

It was time for us to go when our lady coordinator came to me and said, "You will have to take all the collection boxes home with you and sort this money out. I haven't got time. I've got to catch the next train to London. I am going on a Queen cruise". I replied that I didn't know the first thing about sorting the money out, or who to get in touch with. She gave me a phone number and told me to get in touch with the local AIDS group who would tell me what to do, and she was gone.

So I took the money home with me but my day was nowhere near over. I live in a small town in Devon and through a friend of mine who owned a hotel, and had known Screaming Lord Sutch for years, I got to know him myself to a certain degree. So a few weeks prior to our collection day, I had summoned up all my courage and asked him if he felt he could help us with this collection. I was only giving it a try, of course, expecting the answer to be no, but to my great surprise he said, yes, he would help and come out onto the streets with me. He explained that he lived in London but he was quite happy to travel down and be there for us. As the day got closer, he realized he was doing a show in Newcastle the evening before, and it would be impossible to get to us early the next day. But he said, "Don't worry, I'll be there for you, I'll make sure I'm at the hotel in the evening, I'll put on a show for you, and we will raffle one of my books" (he had recently written a book about his life). He said, "Put some adverts out, people will turn up".

So, on the evening of the collection day, I, together with lots of friends and family, went up to the hotel. When we walked in the place was packed, but a big table had been reserved for us. The group started to play their music, but there was no Screaming Lord Sutch. An hour went by, and was I getting embarrassed, feeling I had brought all these people along just to be disappointed. Then, out of nowhere, he appeared, jumped up on to the middle of our table and laughed, saying "You thought I'd forgotten didn't you, you silly woman? I wouldn't have let you down". He then jumped off the table, put his arm around me and said, "This is Mary from the Dairy folks. She is going around spreading AIDS. Oh, sorry, I meant to say trying to help people with AIDS, so let's help her shall we." He knew what he was doing because what he said in a fun way caught everybody's attention. From then on we had a really fun-filled, lovely evening. He presented me with his book; we sold raffle tickets and made over one hundred pounds but it wasn't just the money, it was the caring, it was the fact that he had put himself out for me like that. He was a lovely, lovely man. He was spurring me on, telling me to carry on and he was proud of me. But sadly, as the years went by, although he was full of encouragement, he couldn't keep himself going, and took his own life. What a terrible waste. I will always remember him with love and thanks, and I do hope and pray that like Freddie he is free and happy.

The next day I contacted the AIDS group and was able to sort out the money we'd collected and get it paid into the right account. During my telephone conversation with the manager of this group I asked about the place. Was it run by volunteers? Did they need any volunteers? He confirmed it was run basically by volunteers and asked if I would like to come along and have a chat with him. So I went along, found the place to be a very homely environment and met a few of the people attending that day who were either in various stages of having the HIV virus or they were in the AIDS related part of their illness. They were just there for a coffee and a chat together, and it was good that they could go there, but also I had this feeling that they felt rejected by the majority of the general public. I found this very sad why couldn't people in general be a bit more bighearted about this illness?

Why couldn't they just see that these poor people were going to, more than likely, die in time of their illness? But of course this was 1994; I think there has been a lot of progress made in the treatment available for this virus now and these people have a much better chance of a more fulfilled, longer life. But do people have more understanding about them? I do hope so.

So I became a volunteer. I had to do a thirteen week course first, learning about HIV how you could catch it, how you couldn't catch it. Deciding whether we wanted just to come into the centre and have a coffee and chat with these people; whether we wanted to become a befriender and just be there for one of these people, be their support in a way, be their trusted friend, someone they could rely on. We were told that taking on this role was quite a big responsibility, because if we decided that this was what we wanted it was no good getting involved with someone on a one-to-one basis and then after a couple of months deciding you couldn't be bothered, as that would make the person feel more rejected than ever. I didn't even need to think about this very much as I knew deep in my heart that this was what I wanted to do. Anybody could come into the centre and make tea and coffee and have a chat, but I wanted to go further and give this someone, whoever it may turn out to be, my friendship and my love. These groups don't instantly let you become a befriender. I suppose they like to see what you are like for themselves, how you react to situations. So for a year I just went to the centre, made coffee, sat and chatted to these people, attended their therapy day and was glad to be part of that. I felt that at least I was doing something useful. I kept asking whether there was anybody that would like a befriender. Eventually I was told there was someone who had been in and asked if there was anyone who would like to have a try at being his friend. But I was warned he seemed to be very religious, so they didn't think I would get on with him very well, but I could have a try if I wanted to. So I said was I happy to meet this person and see how we got on. The people at the AIDS centre asked if I would like to get in touch with him personally instead of through them, and I thought this was a good idea. So I phoned him, told him who I was and asked if he would like us to meet. He sounded nice, and he said he was glad I had got in touch with him. His name was Michael, and we arranged to meet, but in this conversation, on my suggestion, we agreed that if we didn't like each other, if we didn't just click somehow, either of us must be brave enough to say so. There was no point in either of us being embarrassed or getting into a situation we didn't feel right about. So it was arranged between us that I would call at his flat for a chat and a cup of tea.

It was a Saturday morning in November 1995. I arrived at 11am, supposedly for about half an hour, but ended up staying with him all day. When I arrived this poor, lost looking person opened the door to me. We were both obviously nervous. It was a dig decision Mike had made to ask for a friend. I gave him a hug, and that relaxed him a bit. Mike was forty-five years old at the time and really just wanting to die, he explained that his illness was so far advanced that if he lived for another three months he would be doing well. But he also said he didn't really care. What was there to live for just emptiness and no one in his life? I found this heartbreaking but of course I didn't tell him this.

I decided I really liked him and he decided he really liked me. As the day went by and Mike felt more at ease talking to me, he revealed something about himself about his feeling that the Lord was walking beside him, trying to give him strength through this bad time. He said he sometimes felt he had arms around him, sometimes he felt there was a presence in the room with him, and that sometimes the Lord conversed with him, and the only way he could explain it to me was that it was like thoughts running through his mind that were not his own. He was completely convinced it was the Lord and I am sure it was.

As he was telling me this story I started thinking that this was almost like what was happening to me, but my experience was not the Lord it was definitely Freddie Mercury. I felt I must be honest and tell Mike about this before the day was through. So I explained that I had had similar experiences but that I was sure mine were coming from a person who up until recently really lived on this Earth and when he passed over had somehow connected up with me. Mike was a bit taken aback by this, obviously, but he suddenly piped up, "I know who this is, it's Freddie Mercury." I asked him how he could possibly know that, and his answer was, "The Lord just told me". But still until this day I wonder if someone at the AIDS centre had told him I collected for the Mercury Phoenix Trust, although he was adamant that he hadn't known about that and it was definitely the Lord giving him this information.

That time spent together certainly bonded us. Mike was convinced we were meant to meet, and said the Lord had sent me to him. By the time I left that day this poor man that I had met only a few hours earlier, definitely seemed at least more relaxed and happy that he had found a friend. We said our goodbyes and hugged each other. We arranged to phone each other the next day, and he said he was very glad that I had turned up on his doorstep.

But the next day was a very different day. I had a phone call from Mike asking me if I would give up Freddie and go over to the Lord with him. I said, no, I was sorry but I couldn't do that, the reason being that I hadn't ever invited Freddie Mercury into my life, so he had obviously chosen me for some reason and if I just blatantly told him to go away and never bother me again, to me, it would be like smacking your best friend across the face. Mike said the trouble was he found it all a bit strange now that he had time to think about it and he didn't know if he could handle it. I told him it was also more than a bit strange to me but had only ever brought good into my life. So I told Mike that I actually found his experience with the Lord travelling beside him a bit strange too. Don't get me wrong, I myself do believe that Jesus lived, but I also had never had a conversation with anyone who believed the Lord was there beside him all the time. So I suggested that if we carried on this friendship we could learn from each other. I could tell him all the things I had experienced since Freddie arrived in my life, and he could tell me about all that had happened, and was still happening to him, where the Lord was concerned. He agreed that it might be a good idea, because he didn't want to lose my friendship just for the sake of something he didn't understand. So we went on from this. Mike and I were very lucky to meet; he became and always will be one of the best friends I have had in my life.

We didn't just talk about the Lord and Freddie all the time. I used to take him shopping and talk to him for hours about his whole life. There were many tears and lots of laughter. I kept his flat clean for him and he cooked meals for me which we sat and shared. He came to stay with my then husband and myself sometimes. And, although some days he was desperately ill, and also had to spend time in hospital, another part of him seemed to wake up and become completely alive. He didn't want to die any more, he wanted to live every one of his good days to the full, and just cope with the bad days as best he could. I spent a lot of the bad days with him; I would visit the hospital and just sit on the bed with him for hours. Sometimes we would talk, sometimes we wouldn't. Mike said he had believed for a long time that when we die that isn't the end of our existence. That part of us our soul or whatever it may be moves on and exists in another dimension, but his worry was that because of the life he had lived being gay, ending up with AIDS, the Lord wouldn't let him sit at his feet. I felt very sad for him why did he have to suffer emotionally like this, thinking he wasn't worthy? I must add that poor Mike had been sexually abused by two of his brothers when he was only a little boy, so you could say they ruined his life, sent him down the wrong track. So why should he have to carry this great guilt? His poor life had been ruined years ago in my eyes. We sat and talked about his worry and I said to him, "Well Mike, if Freddie can be as free as he seems to be, then naturally you are going to be just as free. You won't have to sit by anybody's feet for eternity, you will just be you again, free and well as far as I can see."

After months of these types of conversation together, talking about Freddie, talking about the Lord, talking about everything we could think of, he started to accept that what I was saying must be right, and I would say that 90 per cent of his fear about his life after his death was removed, and it actually gave him something to hold on to that maybe from the other side he would be able to keep in touch with me like Freddie did. He thought that would be wonderful.

Mike also had experiences of having things told to him, just thoughts running through his mind really. He told me one day that he had been told by the Lord that someone who had been very closely connected to Freddie Mercury's life would come to live very close to where Mike's flat was, within walking distance. He said he had been told that it would be a man, and this man would turn up after Mike was no longer with us. I didn't really take this completely on board, because when people, or at least some people, reach the very advanced stages of AIDS, their mind can wander a bit. But I did always remember him saying this. One night, only a few months before Mike died, I had a very vivid dream in which I was sitting by Mike's coffin. He was dressed in a dark grey pinstripe suit and he looked very peaceful. I was talking to him, saying thank you for coming into my life, being my special friend; thank you for the many happy hours we had shared, and for listening to me about Freddie. Then, in my dream, I felt someone standing behind me. It was Mike and he looked so well and happy, and then someone else appeared and it was Freddie, just as well and happy. They both wrapped their arms around me and said, "We are showing you this because you have been so good and caring." Then Freddie said, "Don't ever worry about your friend, I will look after him", and it all faded away. But it was VERY VERY vivid. But the strange thing is, two weeks later I was at Mike's flat, just tidying around for him. He had gone into town, and when he returned he came bouncing in and said, "Look what I've just bought from a charity shop", and out of the bag came a dark grey pinstripe suit. I was completely shocked by the sight of it, but managed to cover this up. I remember saying, "What on earth have you bought that for?" because that was not Mike's way of dressing. He just calmly said, "Oh come on Mary my love, you know what it's for. Now don't go getting yourself upset, we both know I am going to die." He continued, "I tell you what, I'll take you out for a meal soon and I'll wear this suit if that would make you feel better about it". But we never did go for that meal as he was just too ill by then.

My mother became good friends with Mike. We used to call in there and see her sometimes. She knew he had AIDS, but, bless her, she didn't really understand the seriousness of it. Of course she was in her eighties, but she used to say to him, "You don't look all that ill to me, just pull yourself together and beat it, you've got us now." She used to take his face in her hands and say, "Are you listening lad? You've got us now."

Some of my friends became Mike's friends; my daughters became his friends. Two of my daughters came with us to a World AIDS Day church service, and it all gave him courage just because we cared and included him in our lives. All it takes is one person to hold out their hand to someone like that, and you can turn their life around. Mike told me I was the best friend he had ever found. I know I wasn't but, if through that time he thought that, I'm glad I was. If there is anybody out there that feels they could do this for someone, do it. It is best to go on a course first, because that gives you a bit more understanding of the situation. I have never for one second regretted becoming Mike's friend. He injected more into my life that I ever gave him, I can honestly say that.

Mike did have an awareness of things, similar to mine. I would phone him out of the blue, and before I said a word he would say, "Hello my love." I used to say to him, you will say that to the wrong person one day, but his answer was, no I won't because when you phone the Lord says, it's our Mary phoning you. Another thing he used to do was catch hold of me, look me in the eyes and say, "Listen, we have met for more than just friendship. I was sent all the way from Bradford to be able to meet you [he had moved from Bradford two years earlier because of desperate situations in his life which are not relevant to this story] and if you hadn't had this Freddie experience I don't think we would have met... There is another life on the other side of death, so when I get there I will let you know." I told him that if he believed this why didn't he try to find Freddie when he got there, wherever that was.

I promised Mike I would be with him when he died, but actually as the time got closer he went into a hospice and refused to see anyone. So, sadly, he more or less died alone, but it was his choice, and people must have their own rights. He sadly passed away on 5 February 1997, so we had about fifteen months together. I was very upset about the fact I hadn't been there at the end, feeling I should have been stronger and made sure I was there.

About six days later I went to a Spiritualist Church with my twin daughters, who sat either side of me. I don't know what we expected, nothing really, but before the evening was over the medium, who I didn't know, said to me, "I have got a gentleman here for you who used to perform on stage. He says he was a popular singer and he has been your friend from the spirit world for a long time now. He is saying, I have got your friend here who you have just lost. Don't go worrying about him any more, I was waiting for him when he arrived. And your friend is saying, don't feel guilty that you weren't there when I died, it was my wish. Thank you for your friendship, I love you and when I'm stronger. I will come through myself." I just cried and cried, I was so overwhelmed with it all, losing Mike from my life, Freddie being there for him, it was just all too much. Nobody at this church knew anything at all about me befriending someone in this way, so what I was hearing had to be true. Now as the years have gone by and I look back at this situation, I think it's wonderful. It's so comforting to know that your loved ones are safe.

I did go to Mike's funeral, in his home town of Torquay. His funeral was held at St Mathias Church in Wellswood. The flat he had lived in was not far away from the church, and he had told me that he would take some cuttings from his jasmine plant that grew on the wall. He had never got round to doing this, so I went down to the flat after the funeral was over, and took some cuttings, hoping I could make them grow. It would have sparked a nice memory of him, seeing it come back to life each year. But unfortunately each one of them died. I was disappointed about this, but I had something saying to me in my mind: "You are so impatient. You will get your jasmine in the end." I just remember thinking at the time, what's the point of going to a garden centre and buying one, that won't create the same memory, so I never bothered and didn't really think much more about it.

Chapter 4

1997 turned out to be a terrible year. Firstly losing Mike, but of course it is something you must expect when you take on such a commitment. But then, at the end of August 1997, as we all know we lost Princess Diana, and that really rocked the world I am sure.

I must tell you of a small experience I had concerning Diana because, as I see it, it wouldn't be fair to leave it out. On the Monday before Diana died I was watching the television in the evening on my own. As I was watching, a cross and chain appeared across the whole of the television screen. I had never experienced anything like this before and really thought it was my imagination, but it did play on my mind I must admit. Then on the Thursday night I had a very vivid dream, in which I could see two hands coming out of a mist, really I would say maybe out of the spirit world. These hands were holding a beautiful silver tray and on it was a mouldy wedding cake. In my dream I asked my husband, "Can you see that cake?" and he replied "Yes, but don't touch it because it is predicting doom." Then I woke up with a start out of this dream. As I awoke I noticed the clock radio had come on for some reason and it was flashing twelve o'clock. I must admit it really scared me. When I went downstairs that morning our wall clock had stopped just before three am. This worried me all the more for some reason. I don't like clocks stopping like that; I had only wound it up the night before and it never fails to work for at least fifteen days, except this time. Because of my experiences with Freddie I knew I was prone to this type of occurrence but this was scary, not nice at all.

What made it worse was that my husband and I had arranged a short break in London. We were travelling up on Monday 1

September and it was our wedding anniversary the following day. So I was convinced something terrible was going to happen to us and I desperately didn't want to go, but my husband just laughed, saying it was only a silly dream. But then on the Sunday it was announced that Princess Diana had died. The car had crashed at midnight, and she was pronounced dead just before three am. I remember thinking, my God, that's my dream; it was her, that's the disaster we are walking into. How can I have picked up on all this? Are our lives all planned out? Why do these things keep happening to me? I was completely rocked to my very soul by all this the terrible loss of Diana, of course, but also what I had dreamt. Everybody that knew about my dream said how strange it was that I would be in London through this. But we did still go to London, and what an experience it was. Everywhere you went everybody was quiet; all the people were laying flowers at all the palaces; people were crying. You could just feel Princess Diana everywhere, or at least I could. What a terrible, terrible tragedy. Two people's lives snuffed out like that. Because, of course, Dodi Fayed had died as well. So people were gathering around Harrods because of Mohamed Al Fayed's loss as well.

We stayed in London until the afternoon of Friday 5 September, which would have been Freddie's birthday. So I laid some flowers outside his house for him, and then we headed home. We could have stayed for Diana's funeral but I just wanted to get back home and watch it quietly on the television, because it was just all so sad. Of course it would have been so much better if Diana had lived, but I must say I do feel very privileged to have been part of all the activities that were going on in London at that time, experiencing first hand how much people had loved and were going to miss Diana. Everyone at this time, friends and family, were talking to one another about this terrible tragedy saying that nothing worse than this could possibly happen, but before September was through one of our friend's seventeen year old daughter died, with no warning. It was just a terrible time and everybody was broken hearted then sadly, before we could all begin to pick ourselves up from this, my four year old grandson Jake fell into a canal on 18 October. By the time they had found him he had been in the water for about twenty minutes. He was found floating face down by a fisherman. By the time they had managed to get an ambulance to him a long time had elapsed. Someone managed to get him breathing in the meantime, but a couple of times on the journey in the ambulance they almost lost him, but they attached him to a life support machine and flew him up to a special children's hospital in Bristol. They did manage to keep him alive and get him off the life support machine but, because of the time span in the water and the lack of oxygen to his brain, he was left with global brain damage. This means that some of his bodily functions do respond to messages from his brain, unlike in brain stem death, but the control mechanisms that regulate his breathing do not respond as they should so he is prone to chest infections. He is fed by a gastrostomy, a tube into his stomach. He is blind and probably deaf, paralysed and suffers frequent fits. I'm sorry to say this, when I look back at the complete story now, but I am afraid poor old Freddie Mercury went out of the window.

How could anyone possibly believe under such circumstances as these that you have got a stranger linking up to you from the spirit world, let alone a superstar like Freddie Mercury? After three weeks they brought Jake back to his local hospital at Exeter. We all spent as much time as we could with him, because he was expected to die. My poor daughter's life was shattered, and if I had any feelings at all left towards the spirit world, they were certainly not good feelings. Jake defied all the odds and carried on living, and as the months went by none of the specialists was sure now what to do with this little boy, so they suggested to my daughter that if she would be willing to move to another property they would build a specially equipped room on to it for little Jake. They would cater for all his needs, and give twenty-four hour nursing care for him. This is a choice my daughter, Rachel could have if she wanted him home with her. He was her child. So she agreed to move to a flat in another part of Exeter, but when she moved in someone filed an objection to the extension proposal to the back of my daughter's flat. So nothing was done and little Jake, defying all odds, carried on living with no real quality of life, just horrendous chest infections one after the other. The first eighteen months after the accident he lived in hospital, not because they could do anything else for him, but there was nowhere else for him to go. We were all really shattered. They had saved this little boy and they knew it was important especially to my daughter that he was at least listed as belonging somewhere other than a hospital, but I am sure they played on the fact that he wouldn't survive because of his condition. But he did carry on surviving and eighteen months down the line they found him a place to live in a respite centre in Exeter. Jake is still with us, and don't take this the wrong way, because the staff are wonderful with him, but he still hasn't got a permanent home anywhere, because this respite home closes down for the Christmas period. So every year my grandson has to go back into hospital for this period. They have suggested Jake could have a permanent home completely out of the county, which my daughter refused, thank God, so this is how it all stands at the moment. So this is, just briefly, our story of Jake. I am making a point of telling you this, with my daughter's permission, so that you can all see that at that time I couldn't possibly believe in all this about Freddie Mercury. Now I will explain how Freddie came back into my life. I don't actually think he ever left; he just waited patiently in the background.

In April 1998 I had a phone call from a friend, saying guess who's moved to Torquay. I said I didn't have a clue, but she was all excited and said Peter Freestone. I hadn't got a clue who Peter Freestone was, and really didn't care; all I cared about at the time was Jake. But she explained to me that he had been Freddie's personal assistant for many years, and of course everyone the fans who liked Queen and Freddie thought it was wonderful. So I just said, "Oh that's nice for you all", and left it at that. But then I learned that the hotel Peter Freestone had bought was only five minutes' walk away from where my friend Mike's flat had been. So things started moving around in my mind again, about all that had happened with Freddie. Had Mike really heard that voice telling him these things after all? If it was a coincidence that this person had bought a hotel so close to where Mike lived, it was definitely a big one. Then I was thinking, my God, I hope this isn't the person Freddie told me about all those years ago. Surely I hadn't got to take the message I was told to him. But I disregarded it all because, after all, I had been told the person would be someone who Freddie regarded as his family and this man wasn't family. I thought, therefore it was nothing to do with me, so I just concentrated on Jake. And also around July 1998 Rachel realized she was pregnant, so at the time, that was a concern as well, but this child was coming into the world, and that was that. I spent a lot of time with Rachel at the hospital. Afterwards we would have something to eat together in the hospital restaurant. Rachel was adamant that she wanted a boy, and the possibility of a girl never came into the conversation. But one day we were halfway through a meal when she suddenly said, "If I have a girl, Mum, I am going to call her Jasmine. And it rushed into my mind Jasmine that's what had been told to me after Mike died, and Rachel had never heard anything about the story of the jasmine plant. So why had this name Jasmine come to her? I covered up my feelings well, because I didn't want to frighten or upset her in any way. Then she said, "I'll probably have a boy anyway".

Rachel was due to have this child on 6 March but as the time got closer she wasn't well at all, and kept being taken into the hospital with false alarms, so there was no way she would get to 6 March before the child arrived. But I was told during this time by a medium one night (I mean a medium that knew nothing about myself or my family) that the spirit world was telling her that my eldest daughter was carrying a child at the moment, that it would be a girl, and that she would be born on 6 March. I remember saying that she couldn't possibly go on that long, but this woman was adamant, saying "Your daughter will have this child on 6 March.

Now, cutting a long story short, my daughter did have her child on this date 6 March 1999, and it was a girl and she called her Jasmine. So it was true what I heard because, as I was told, I have now got my Jasmine.

Rachel now knows this story about what I heard, and she thinks it's amazing, but doesn't understand it. It is hard to understand, I know that. I don't even understand it all myself. Anyway, some friends of mine who were very into Queen, and had been for years, got to know this Peter Freestone well. They told me he was a very nice person, and really he was part of what Freddie had considered his family, because he was one of the people who had always been there for Freddie. They suggested I might like to meet him, it might cheer me up, give me something else to think about. But I didn't want to meet him, I didn't want to do anything, my frame of mind at the time could only ask the question: why should I have a life, when my grandson couldn't?

Chapter 5

My friends did persuade me at least to go to a show that was being put on in Torquay. It was a group called the Royal Family, a kind of tribute to Queen. It was August 1998, and that night I met Peter Freestone myself and he was lovely. He shook my hand, gave me a hug, said it was nice to meet me, and he would see me again. Something reopened up inside me that night; this man had given me a hug why would he bother to hug me? He had been part of the superstar Freddie Mercury's life and I started to wonder whether Freddie really was staying close to me through all this troubled time after all.

Shortly afterwards I went to a barbeque at Peter's hotel. We had a nice chat together, in which I told him about my grandson, and he told me bits about Freddie, but not Freddie's stardom, just more really about how he still missed him. By now, I had started to think whether this was the man Freddie said I would meet. Should I really give him the message I had held inside all these years. But even if it was, how could I? You can't just suddenly pipe up, oh by the way Freddie wants me to say...! He would have just thought I was mad. So I kept it to myself, and just enjoyed the fact I had met him. And it was making me more sociable again, seeing my friends a bit more often.

In November 1998 there was a masked ball held at Peter's hotel, so we went along to it. Peter looked very smart in his suit; everyone had made an effort, and we all had a good time, but I'm afraid it all got too much for me, because I still thought I shouldn't be enjoying a social life when my very young grandson was trapped in such an awful situation. So as I got a bit tipsy as the evening wore on, I seemed to wander away from the rest of the people, completely lost in my own thoughts, and Peter came over to see me. He just gently pulled me into his kitchen and closed the door. He put his arms around me and said, "Come on just cry it all out." I remember saying, "I can't, what about your lovely suit." He replied, "I really don't care about my suit", so I just gave in and cried and cried. I expect I muttered and mumbled all sorts of rubbish to him but he just patiently listened and held me close. And then he said, "Come on, dry your eyes, let's go back to the others now." We went back and joined the others and he just stood calmly with his arm round my shoulders for a while, until I had pulled myself together. No one else at the party realized what had taken place. He is such a caring man, how could I ever thank him.

As the weeks went by I started to see life differently. Peter was having to live a different life without Freddie and carry on, so what right had I got to continue on wallowing in my misery like this. I had heard about this nice little Spiritualist Centre at St Marychurch just outside Torquay so decided to go. It turned out that the same person who had given me the message, years ago, about this man who had died in London and completely changed my life, had set up the centre and, if you remember my mentioning this earlier in the book, I denied it and he just moved on to someone else. This is the same man who has since sat with me for many long hours and helped to get Freddie through for me to tell us lots of things for this book. And now I am very proud to say that his name is Keith Hall, who is a very well-known and loved international medium. And, through all our experiences, he knows without a doubt that this is Freddie coming through. I am very lucky to have him as my friend. I would never doubt him for one second; everything he brings through from the spirit world is definitely genuine.

This is not the only way that Keith has helped me. He got to know the story of my grandson, and he asked me if there was one thing I could have, where Jake was concerned, what would it be. I said just to let hem know that we all care because I just had this feeling that Jake had some sort of awareness. Keith said, "I'll do that for you. I'll tune into his mind for you. Let's see what he's got to say." I remember saying, "You can't do that, he's not dead." But Keith said to me, "There's a lot of things you don't understand about this movement, my love. You don't always have to be dead. If someone gets trapped in their body, the way your grandson has, someone like myself can tune into his mind, his spirit. His spirit is still there you know. Would you like us to have a go, and see what happens?" So what could I lose, I thought, and agreed, not believing anything could happen, of course. But the things that came through were amazing. Only things that Jake could know about, reams of it. He told Keith his spirit was free, and often travelled around with me, because I was open to this type of thing. He knew what everything looked like, where I worked at the time, and he said he watched us moving the furniture around, which is what was happening at the time. He said he could see the fields around this house were filled with snowdrops, and they were, and he said that when I looked at his body, please don't cry so much, just try to see what was inside. He told us many more things, which were definitely right. He told us so much more, but I am not going into it any deeper here, because it upset my daughter. She thought it wasn't fair; if anybody were able to connect up to him it should be her, and she couldn't, and I understood. He's her son not mine. So we don't delve into all of this, but Jake does sometimes say something to Keith, and he passes it on to me, and time I am sure will tell this story. This was early in 1999, time has gone by now, and maybe my daughter now feels differently about all this, but we don't really discuss such things where Jake is concerned.

In early March 1999, Peter laid on a Mother's Day lunch, which we all enjoyed. He gave all the mothers a gift a picture frame. Well of course I put Freddie in it who else? By this time I knew in my heart of hearts that somehow I was going to have to tell this story to him about Freddie. But how? So that day when we were all chatting together I threw into the conversation a little bit about spiritualism, just to see Peter's reaction really. He didn't seem to react with shock and horror, but I didn't push it too far, and we just all had a nice few hours together. But after this day it felt as if something was, I would say, moving a bit closer to me, trying to make me feel obligated to come out with this story.

Then I had a very vivid dream, in which I went into a big, empty house. In the house there was a flight of steps, which seemed to rise from the centre of a big hallway. At the top of these steps there was a balcony you could stand on and look back down into the hallway. I opened one of the upstairs doors, and all that was in the room was a table and Freddie was leaning against it looking terribly disappointed or sad about something. He didn't look up at me, he just completely ignored me. So I shut the door again quickly, and as soon as I had shut it I thought, I've really let this person down after all that he had brought into my life. So I opened it again to say something to him, but he had gone. I can still remember this dream as clearly in my mind now as when it happened. And I really feel he was trying to show me how disappointed he was. So I summoned up all my courage and went to see Peter.

But before I continue with this story I must stress the fact that my only intention in writing this book is to bring hope and some sort of contentment into people's lives in the assurance that we do live on after this life on Earth is over. I believe this completely, but if some of you can only find hope that we do then that will make me happy that I plucked up the courage to write it.

So I sat quietly and told Peter this story of mine, up until now. I told him I was sure that I was meant to tell him this, that Freddie would continue to pester me until I gave in and spoke out. I told him the message I had carried in my heart. I can't tell you all what this message was as that wouldn't be fair. It was for him alone. Not even for me, I was just the messenger. After I had told him I expected him to say, "Get out you stupid woman, and don't ever bother me again." But he did exactly the opposite. He said he really liked me, he thought I was very genuine, he believed that I believed this story, and thanked me for telling him. He said he had an open mind to these things, but hadn't experienced anything like this at all himself. However he said that he could see some sense in this message for him. I can never tell you all how relieved I was. I really thought that he would just go mad, and say how dare you ridicule Freddie like this. I actually do think that this message did give Peter some comfort and thank God if it did.

I also do believe that this message was for all three men who looked after Freddie so well throughout his illness and right up until the end of his life. Of course Freddie would have been able to tell the person Joe himself, because I don't think that it was long after Freddie died that Joe also passed away.

I did meet Jim Hutton once briefly. I went with some friends up to London on 24 November 1995 just to experience being outside Freddie's house on the anniversary of his death, just to be with the rest of the people, to see how they reacted really. I'm glad I went, it was an experience. But to me, of course, Freddie is as free as a bird, so you don't need to go to certain places to find him. He will come to us when he wants to.

Anyway, going back to Jim, he was standing on the corner with some fans around him, not by Freddie's house. I found this very sad surely he should have been invited into the house, rather than standing there in the street? I went over to him after a while and said, "Come and stand with the rest of us. You belong here more than us. Don't stay in the background." He replied that he couldn't make himself stand outside the house and he was okay because the fans came over to him. I couldn't bear this remember I wasn't a Queen fan standing there. I wasn't seeing this through their eyes. I just saw this man who seemed to feel rejected for some reason. So I managed to persuade him away from the fans and we had a quiet chat together, and I told him also briefly about my Freddie experiences. He replied that actually he had also felt closer to Freddie sometimes since he had passed over than when Freddie was alive. He said he was very happy to meet me, and hoped we would see each other again. I have never seen him again, but I am very glad I met him that day.

I became good friends with Peter. I would call in on him sometimes on his invite, not just being a nuisance. And I became very fond of him, and this feeling of fondness for him was actually nothing to do with meeting him because of Freddie; although of course I would never have met him if it wasn't for Freddie. I called him my special person; to me he was, and always will be because, apart from this Freddie Mercury experience, Peter is the one who turned me around when I didn't really know how to get on with living again because of my grandson Jake.

I must just tell you this little story, because it's special to me. My then husband and I and two friends went to see an Abba tribute band at our local theatre and Peter and his friend happened to be there. And don't get this all wrong, because I was with my husband for fifteen years and he was a good husband, although thoughtless at times, but then we all have faults. Anyway, we were all queuing to get into the theatre, and Peter and his friend were standing by me. As we all went in Sam, my husband, held the door open for our friends, went in himself and the door smacked back into me. I remember looking at Peter and saying, "Well, that says it all doesn't it?" He just laughed and gave my shoulder a hug. Peter and his friend didn't sit with us, they sat at the back. When the show was over, and everybody started to leave the theatre, I could see Peter and his friend just standing there waiting while all the people passed them, and when I got up to him he wrapped his arms round me and gave me a big hug. He didn't say anything he just hugged me, so did his friend. And I'm sure it was just their kindness and caring for what they had seen happen earlier.

The following night we were going to Exeter with my daughter Rachel, Jake's mum, to see a group called Mercury, because for some time now my daughter had become very interested in Freddie. She said she felt it brought some sort of comfort into her life, and sometimes I must say I did wonder whether Freddie had moved in close to her to try to help her through this bad time in her life. I asked Peter and his friend if they would like to join us. It certainly wouldn't be like watching Queen to Peter, but I was sure it would be a sociable event. So I gave them the name of the pub in Exeter, the wrong name, I must tell you, which we all had a laugh about later. But Peter had tracked it down and he was there waiting for us when we arrived. It was a lovely surprise to see them and we had a really good night. Rachel, myself and Peter's friend Martin stood at the front of the other people, close to the group, and Martin kept his arm around Rachel's waist. I am sure it was his way of comforting her. What was it Freddie said, dear old ladies, still rocking away? That was me. We all knew the words to the songs and we sang and danced around. It is a wonderful memory to me.

I must add this to the story. Soon after I had plucked up courage to tell Peter all this about Freddie something really amazing happened. I walked into this small Spiritualist Centre at St Marychurch one evening and a man who was sat close to the doorway said, “Hello, did you two enjoy your journey here?” I said, “Yes thank you”, thinking that someone had walked in directly behind me, and he had just took it for granted that we were together. But this man said to me, “I mean you and your spirit friend.” I asked him what he meant by that, and he replied casually, “Oh, I have got psychic abilities, I can see spirits sometimes, and a man from the spirit world has walked in with you.” He was adamant that as the evening wore on I would be told about this man by the medium. The medium that night was a lady called Brenda Sawyer. A very trusted lady, she has been a medium for years and definitely doesn’t make up silly stories. As the evening wore on, sure enough this lady said to me, “You have got a gentleman from the spirit world sitting beside you dear. You have actually got another gentleman from the spirit world sat on the other side of you, but it is the first one I mentioned who really wants to make you understand who he is. He is saying, I purposely came here with this lady tonight, I came to tell her something very important. I will say who I am if I need to but I don’t want to draw unwanted attention to this lady, she has got enough upset to cope with.” The medium carried on and said, “This gentleman is saying, tell her I passed away on 24 November and she will know who I am, tell her that I have come here tonight to say thank you for caring about me and giving me her love, and I will never leave her. But tell her I also know that she worries about her friend who is here with me, who she looked after so well on Earth. She worries because she thinks we are not happy. I watch her laying in bed at night thinking please be happy you two. He said I want her to understand that we are very happy. We just keep in touch because we care for her. But she mustn’t worry about us the way she does, we are fine.” Then the spirit person, who was obviously Freddie said via the medium, “Tell the lady in one year’s time we will find a special person for her, someone she can love, and will love her”. This was in March 1999. I was overwhelmed by this message; the other person was obviously Mike, but I couldn’t see anybody sitting by me.

I had somewhere along the way given Peter a crystal, a blue star, and said to him, “Why don’t you hang it in your hotel somewhere where the sunlight will catch it, and when it throws a ray of colour across the room just think of Freddie." He did look at me a bit oddly but said, "Thank you, that's a kind thought". I also had 'A Winter's Tale' printed out for him and put it in a frame with a picture of Freddie from his 'Slightly Mad' song. Like myself, I thought, slightly mad. I also put a butterfly in the picture frame, because, I don't know if you know, but butterflies represent free spirits. Again he said thank you. A while after this I went to a special party at Peter's hotel, and while I was there he said, "Come with me a minute." In his kitchen he had hung the crystal in the window and the song was on the wall. I was so happy about this, not for me, for him. He said he liked to see them there every day.

Sadly, seeing Peter on a regular basis came to an abrupt end that night, and I am sure that what happened was planned by Freddie. I am sure he must have had an overpowering influence on people when he was on Earth, because he has definitely got one now. It was one year down the line, to the month, that Freddie said he would find someone for me.

Chapter 6

We were all gathered at a farewell party for someone at Peter's hotel. We had been there for about half an hour when this man walked in. We seemed instantly to catch each other's eye. I remember thinking, who is that, I haven't seen him before?

As the evening wore on this person and I got chatting more than we should have done, I'll be the first to admit. At the end of the evening we exchanged phone numbers, so that this man Norman and his partner, and myself and my husband could keep in touch. But it didn't work out like that. Norman and I became besotted with each other and before we knew it we were together. Leaving my husband so quickly after meeting Norman caused a lot a upset and heartbreak at the time, for myself also, but time has gone on now and everybody has settled into their new lives. But one thing I must stress is that if I had stayed with my husband I would never have written this book. He couldn't understand my Freddie Mercury experiences over the years. I didn't really talk to him very much about it and I must say he was very good about it, but I am sure he never believed it, and who can blame him really. But Norman does believe it; although he has had no choice really, because it is since I have been with Norman that Freddie has started coming through with things more often, and in a completely different way, and Norman has witnessed a lot of this himself. Also Mike has come through to me in his own right.

Norman started coming to the Spiritualist Church with me, and initially we got combined messages, saying the people in the spirit world had been watching us, and they were glad we were together at last. A couple of weeks later we were at the church and there was a medium from up country somewhere. Through the course of the evening he said, "I have got a Michael here. He is calling out I am Michael, can anybody claim him?" Mike used to like being called Michael so I said, yes, I knew someone by that name, so maybe it was for me. And this gentleman medium walked over to me. They don't usually do that; they usually stay at the front of the church. But he said he just had to come down to me. He said, "This Michael in the spirit world is saying I have been waiting for this opportunity, so you can go and tell the lady for me that I can come through myself now and I want to say thank you for being my special friend on Earth, thank you for reaching out to me, and giving me your love. I was such an emotional wreck on Earth that even though you did give me hope and your caring [and I did treasure that] I was never really completely emotionally healed when I left the Earth, but I want you to know that I am now fine and happy. I know how much you wanted to be with me when I passed away, but it was my choice, you mustn't feel guilty. I saw you at my funeral and thank you for the red rose" [I had put a red rose on his coffin]. He said many more things but I just want you all to see how clearly they can come through to you from the spirit world if they want to and of course they can communicate better with a professional medium.

I introduced Norman to my friend Keith, and we went to his home one evening so that he could do a reading for us. For anyone who doesn't understand what a reading is, you spend maybe an hour with a medium and they link in to the spirit world for you. Anyone who has passed over to the other side, members of your family, loved ones, friends, anyone really who you knew, can, if they want to, say what they want you to know through their communication with the medium.

Through this reading we got messages, Norman and I, from close relatives really and then suddenly Keith said, "I have got Freddie Mercury here. He is saying tell her this is Freddie with her and has been all along. Tell her I want her to start writing things down for me. Tell her I am often with her and see what she is doing and I want to thank her for lighting the candle for me."

I was completely taken aback by all this because the day before I had visited a place called Buckfast Abbey and I had lit a candle, and as I lit it I had said, "This is for you Fred, only you."

The whole reading had been taped, so I could listen to it all again when I got home, but what was even stranger was that when I listened as Freddie started coming through, you could hear a heartbeat on the tape. This was 15 December 2000. But then something strange happened the next day. I just had this overpowering feeling that I had to write down these things that were rushing into my head; words, rhymes just flowing quickly into my mind.

But before I go on any further I must tell you that over the previous months I had slowly put together a poem for Peter. It was hard work and didn't come to me easily. It was just a thank you to Peter, something for him to treasure; and my original idea was to hold on to it have it, printed out and framed, and then take it to him on the tenth anniversary of Freddie's passing away. This is that poem:

My thank you to Freddie and Peter

When you lived on this Earth
You were famous,
A star in everyone's eyes.
But sadly they lost you,
or so it would seem,
But I know that our soul simply flies.
We go off to a different horizon
And we leave all the bad things behind.
And we look down on this Earth,
And we see from above
The ones who were true or unkind.

There's someone on this Earth
You love dearly.
Although how much, he perhaps never knew.
But we've found him,
And told him between us,
Now I'm sure that he knows
This is true.

So I hope he will treasure this wonderful thing,
The story unfolded,
The love that it brings.

And thank you dear Freddie
For the love I've received,
I'm sorry it took me so long to believe.
But I know you're safe now,
And happy not sad,
That your life is eternal,
And that makes me glad.

I love you dear Freddie,
But how can I explain
All that stands in the way, is your name.
Because you were famous,
They say, how could you find me.
And that's were it's hard.
People don't want to see.
If you were an auntie, an uncle, a friend,
There's a few who might start
To believe in the end.

But whatever this is,
I'm glad you came to my life.
You've helped me stand tall,
Through much trouble and strife.
So Dear Freddie Mercury whatever you are,
Always remember, you're my shining star.

Now your friend is my friend,
But how can that be?
There are times when I think
That you sent him to me
When I was falling apart.
And I know that this caring
Came straight from his heart.

So thank you for sending
Dear Peter my way.
I treasure these things,
And think of you Every Day.

But obviously, now I look back at it all, Freddie had different ideas than waiting around for ten years to pass. He had managed to get my attention more fully now, because of what had come through Keith and the heartbeat on the tape, because to me his very presence was pulsating away on that tape.

So going back to 16 December 2000, this is what I managed to write down very rapidly:

The wind is blowing strongly
All around your head,
There are children out there crying
And there's people to be fed.

But upon the horizon,
The sun is shining bright,
And things just come together,
And every thing's all right.
And this is where it started,
My life just turned around.

This came through to me, at about 6.30 am in a very short space of time, just a few short minutes. I was completely bewildered. Where has that come from, I remember thinking. But before the day was out, this other poem came through:

On Earth I was just famous,
Now I'm more than you could know
And I want to share it with you,
Because others need to know.

Our life on Earth is short in time,
But this goes on forever.
An eternal time, when you're free as a bird,
And I will leave you never.

We've come a long way, you and I,
And you always kept your promise
And your times were hard, I know all this
But I still knew you would do this.

You're right I did send Peter,
Because I knew you would go to him.

(There is a section in this poem that is very personal and I don't think it is right for me to put it into this book, but now I will carry on and tell you the rest.)

And it has been a strange time for you.
This I clearly understand.
A superstar coming into your life
But I'll never let go of your hand.

But now please let's move forward,
Because there's more that I need to say,
Tell Peter I care for him, all of the time,
And I'll never go away.
But there's so much more that I want you to know
About how things are over here,
About the peace that I've found,
And the hope that I've got,
Because there's nothing here to fear.

So this is just the beginning,
And I've sent it on in a rhyme,
Just to get you used to going with the flow.
But things will become clearer with time.
So don't give up, hold on, keep calm,
Things soon will be coming your way.

You think that I've led you a merry dance,
But I won't let you down.
I will stay.

So of course I was excited as well by now. This poem had come to me within ten minutes and even then I must say I wasn't completely convinced it was coming from Freddie, but it was definitely coming from somewhere out there.

So now I couldn't wait for the ten years either, so I phoned Peter and asked him if he would like a copy of the tape. He said that would be nice, just for curiosity's sake. So on Christmas Eve 2000 I called in at Peter's hotel and gave him the two poems, a copy of the tape and a candle, and I asked him if he would light it for me on Christmas Day, because Freddie would know. He said he would do that, so I came away quite happy and thought that must be what Freddie wanted me to write for him, and now he would be happy. But I was very wrong on that one; up until now I have had about sixty-five of these poems coming through. Some of them are very personal to me, as though just to be comfort to me, if maybe I am upset or wondering about something I can't really work out for myself. A lot of them are like little stories really, just making it obvious that he can see me and what is going on around me. I will share a few with you, as the story goes on.

Christmas Day came and went and then I started to think, I will have a real hard go at this trying to talk to Freddie. I thought, I will just sit quietly somewhere, with a writing pad at the ready and write down anything that comes into my head even if it is rubbish. So on 1 February 2001 I found a quiet place to sit, where there was no chance of any disturbance and I said, "Well come on Freddie, this is your golden opportunity. I expected nothing, but this is what I got. My first question was "What is it that you would like me to do for you Freddie?"

This is the answer, and if you readers are amazed you are not anywhere near as amazed as I was at the time. It started with:

I would like you to prove through me that life goes on after we have passed from this Earth. I would like you to be strong and say that it is me with you guiding you on with this, and I also know what you want to say back to me, that people won't believe us but it is time that we stepped out of this nonsense now. I have given you so much evidence in every way possible to prove to you that it has got to be me with you and I have also sent as much love to you as I possibly could, surely you can see that. Look back at the things that have happened at Peter's hotel to change things for you. People think that I am not there but I am. You are wasting your talents, Mary. You need a quieter more fulfilled life and then, you wait and see, you will fly with the best of them. Why do you think your medium friend Keith seems to be looking into your soul sometimes when he looks at you. It is because he can see it all around you.

So now I ask another question. The question is: "Do you ever see my friend Mike, because to me he was definitely a stepping stone in all of this?" Now this is what came back to me:

Mike and I have many a chat and are the best of friends. He still loves you dearly and is often around you. But he has taken a step back because he knows I need to come closer to you now. Because things are coming together and the time will soon be right. But you must know that I found Mike for you for that short time. Look how you turned him around and made sure that he believed the truth and not what he was afraid of. Remember the time that you said to me that you wished you could, just once, give me a hug to thank me for all that I had done for you and I told you that you could for a while, through the time you would be able to spend with Mike, and you talked to him about this that you had heard, but it scared you both really I know, but you will find out when you come back home, whenever that is, that that is how thing are. Sometimes we reach out through others to you and you really haven't got anything to be afraid of in the future with all this. I have tried to tell you so many times in different ways that I will always be with you but I know that you doubt that and think it is just your hopes. That is why I have said it through your medium friend, that this is me because surely you believe him. I also will say to you that I wouldn't really have liked to say in a church to you that this is Freddie Mercury, mainly because people would scorn this and I wouldn't want to put you in that position. But that doesn't mean that I wouldn't say this in a small group of people who do believe these things. But, anyway, look back to the beginning of all this did we need any help from others to find each other? No, it just happened and I know that you have always known this from the very first moment that it was true. Just VERY VERY hard to understand.

So this was my first success, shall we call it, in being able to listen to what Freddie wanted to say to me, and I will explain about the hugging bit. One day I just said to Freddie that I wished I could just be able to give him one big hug for all the things he had brought into my life. This is when I was a befriender to Mike and I heard someone say, "You can while Mike's around." Mike and I talked about everything together so I told him about this and I do remember us both feeling a bit strange about it. It wouldn't worry me so much now though, because as time, as gone on I have learned more about how the spirit world can reach us. And now, looking back on all the things that have happened with this Freddie experience, I can almost see the pattern of the story falling together over the years.

My friend Keith Hall, who is now happy to be named, was the one who told me all those years ago that this man who died in London had completely changed my life. I denied it, knowing that it was true. Then I never saw this man again for years until after my grandson had had his accident. So he was then able to give me comfort to a certain degree about that situation in our lives. Then I met Peter Freestone. Later I met Norman at Peter's hotel. Norman believes all this about Freddie; my husband didn't.

Since I have been with Norman something new seems to have opened up in me that has made it easier for me to communicate with the spirit world, and anything deep that Freddie wants to say Keith can catch on to better than me. But I must add this: I would say Freddie, or the spirit of Freddie, is also very lucky to have found us because he has quite blatantly told us that he probably wouldn't have bothered with us when he lived on Earth. And he has told Keith that he only comes through to him because he wants to get the messages to me. So I will just say this before I go on with this story, I am very fond of you Freddie but you can be a bit too honest sometimes.

I will add a few of the poems I received just for you to see there seems to be a story in them. It was about 17 February 2001 that this poem came through:

When I look down on Earth,
From where I stand now.
I see everything so crystal clear.
About all the reasons, my life seemed so short.
About all of my hopes, and my fears.
My fear was always I wouldn't find love.
My hopes were, I'd make people see.
I came for a purpose,
My voice was a gift.
I reached out and made myself known,
But I never knew living a life such as this
Would make me feel so alone
I was famous I know that,
And loved by the crowds,
But inside I always seemed lost.
So the life that I lived,
And the way that I was,
In the end, I just paid the cost.
But I wasn't unhappy,
For all of my life.
My music and songs were my life.
I spent many years in the clouds in a dream,
Thinking I was really the one.
Because people adored me,
And they seemed to love me,
But from a distance, was all they could see.

But people seemed to prefer it like this,
They said that it might change my image
Of what they wanted to hear and to see,
If they finally met me.
It hurt at first, but I learned to accept,
That this was the easiest, this was the best.
Then there would be no disappointment of my image on stage,
Because my image on stage, it wasn't really me.
When I stepped up there, I was a different man.
Whereas off the stage, I was private,
Liked to spend the time alone.
But don't get this all wrong,
I led a full life
And although it was short,
It was well worth the strife.

Chapter 7

In late February 2001 I went to see Keith for a reading. One of the reasons I go for these readings now and again is really more in the hope that little Jake just might tell us something. So in a way it's still a surprise to me that Freddie comes through to me so easily. But don't get this wrong, I'm not trying to push him away; I like to hear these things from him. I'm just still always surprised that he wants to talk to me.

Anyway I was told different things that Freddie could see me doing. For instance I had acquired a picture of Freddie. Very shortly before this, Norman and I had gone with my daughter Rachel to see a group called Ga Ga. After the show they had a stall, selling different items. On this stall there was two sketches of Freddie so Norman bought one of them for me, and one for Rachel. Freddie said he had seen us there and saw us buy these pictures of him. He said also that he was very aware of Jake and my daughter's problems concerning her son and that he is around her sometimes just trying to give her comfort.

I must explain something to you all. It may seem as the story progresses that I only get messages from Freddie through Keith now. This isn't true. If I make an effort to go to spiritual evenings I still get messages relating to this situation from other mediums. For example, a different message like, "Why don't you get on with your book a bit quicker, you have two to write you know". I don't know what this next one is supposed to be about, but if there is going to be another one I expect time will tell that. And also Keith is a very busy man who is hardly ever home, so you catch him when you can. And there are no long discussions with Keith in-between our meetings, so he certainly isn't picking these messages up through conversations we have shared. These things coming through are genuine, not fantasy.

Shortly after one visit to Keith this poem came through:

Now you can see,
My very special friend.
I told you all along,
I would stay until the end.
And how could I see,
Your picture on the wall,
If I didn't come and visit,
If I wasn't there at all?
At last we've found someone maybe
Who will help us get together.
I've been waiting for a chance like this
I said I'd leave you never.
And please go and tell your daughter,
That I visit her a lot.
I just try to help to ease her pain,
Because of all the worries she has got.
I'm quite aware of Little Jake,
And the trouble that he's in.
And I know how much it breaks your heart,
When you think of what might have been.
You didn't think I'd leave you did you
When you have helped me the way you did?
Of course I'll help your daughter,
She's part of you my dear,
And while she's got this worry
Tell her I will always stay real near.
Just look at how we've started connecting up.
Through our friend
Keith who is there when we call.
If it wasn't for him
I don't really think
You would ever have believed at all,
That a person like me Freddie Mercury
Could ever come into your life.
But that's not what I am,
That's just what I was.

And sometimes it cuts like a knife,
That people try to connect to me,
So they can brag about my name,
That's all that they want,
But won't get it from me.
It's just people like you,
Who are special you see.
You just gave me your love,
Helped with my pain.
And I'll come and I'll visit again and again.

At the time that this poem came through there had been no mention of my writing a book. I just was amazed I was getting what I was getting. It's only as time has gone on that I was told or asked really if I would write this book. But as I am putting things together I myself can see elements in these poems that even then were leading up to this book. I'm sure it was just preparing me to put all this together for you people to see for yourselves.

I never received any poems or anything really again until 31 July 2001. So, as you can all see, my contact with Freddie Mercury in the spirit world has never been an ongoing, day to day experience in my life.

Chapter 8

31 July 2002.

Once upon a time,
there was a man and this girl.
Everything moved slowly,
all in a whirl.
And before they knew it,
Their life had been taken.
And they were left standing hopeless
Disappointed and shaken.
Then out of the blue,
They met once again.
And their life has gone crazy
Ever since then.
And you know who it is,
It's you and your friend.
But this is the start,
It isn't the end.
You just see all the worry,
The hurt and the stress.
But don't worry sweetheart,
Because that will become less.
Soon you will fly, as free as a bird
And one thing I'm sure of,
Your voice will be heard.
And I will stay with you,
I promise you this.
And Mike will be there too,
And sends a hug and a kiss.
And we both say, be strong now,

Don't ever give in.
Because we can see you so clearly,
And we know you will win.
Life becomes heavy, sometimes we know.
But all you must do, is go with the flow.

I have had this poem explained to me by someone who understands these things better than myself, and they say this is about Norman and me, in a previous life together, and something took our lives quickly. Maybe it is, but I must say although I do believe in reincarnation I am not very deeply interested in it.

My mother then passed away at the age of ninety on 4 September 2001 so I will tell you all briefly now about my mum. She was the best friend to me anyone could ever have, and I hope I was to her. My father left us soon after I was born so I was brought up by my mother and my grandmother. But I am certainly not complaining; it bonded the three of us really close together. I always tried to be there for both of them I am the only child because they were always there for me. My gran passed away when I was twenty-six so that made my mother and I even closer really.

When Freddie started moving into my life, I always told my Mother every single thing that happened and I can honestly say, she never once said that it couldn't be true and I must be imagining it. She always listened to what I told her, she seemed intrigued actually, and if there was anything at all on the television or in the papers about Freddie she never missed any of it. I think it actually brought pleasure into her life and took away her fear of dying. My mother never remarried; I think my father really broke her heart. But the one thing that strangely does give me comfort is that she died on 4 September, the day before what would have been Freddie's birthday. She had a very peaceful death, and in view of what was wrong with her she shouldn't have. But I just feel, as silly as it sounds, that Freddie said, "Come on mum, come home to us now, you've had enough of that earthly life, come and join my celebrations." So I hope now that she is really happy and having a good time.

I have had messages sent through to me from her saying that she is really happy now. Another strange thing is I always for all those years since my gran died worried about her was she alright? was she lonely? but I don't worry about her at all now. To me it is like life has gone round in a big circle and they are now reunited.

On 8 October I received this poem, which proves to me that they are being sent to me, because I could never have made this up so shortly after the death of my mother. So here it is:

Freddie Mercury was my name,
And it brought me wealth and fame.
But underneath I was just me,
Just one more person longing to be
Loved and cared for, cherished and caressed
And yes you could say it brought me the best.
There was love in abundance,
Or so it would seem.
But where was the person
I saw in my dreams.
You see that person I saw,
Did not really exist.
She was just there in my thoughts
Somehow lost in a mist.
But I found many people,
Lots of love, lots of care.
But the one that I wanted,
Was never quite there.
But I always had this feeling
Life on Earth was not quite true.
Not something I could tell you,
Just something I just knew.
But when I passed over
my God it was true.
I was still here alive, but nobody knew.
I saw people crying devastated that I'd gone.
But how could I tell them,
That I'd only moved on?
Then I saw your light shining,

And I thought she will know.
But how can I reach her,
How can she go with my flow?
Then to my amazement,
You seemed instantly there,
And I felt all this love,
And I felt all this care.
At last someone special,
Had caught hold of my hand,
Although you couldn't see this,
How could you understand?
And I led you down strange roads
Never letting you go.
Hoping you would see,
Hoping you would know.
Hoping you'd be brave, and face this great thing.
Hoping you could feel, All the love it would bring.

And yes you fulfilled this,
You never let me go.
And because of your love,
Other people got to know
That I didn't just die,
It wasn't a waste.
My time down on Earth
Was only a taste
Of something eternal,
That will always go on.
And for the rest of forever,
You'll be the one
Who stood strong and solid,
Went to Peter for me,
Made him believe and made him see
That I was sorry, so sorry,
That things had gone wrong.
And with thanks for this love,
I'll try to send you a song.

So when you're lonely or sad,
Don't ever let go.
Because I'll never leave you,
By now you should know.
But to receive this new song,
You must try very hard,
And anything you hear
You mustn't disregard.
It might take a while
But will be there in the end.
It will be something to treasure,
For just you my friend.

Freddie has told Keith and myself that he has tried to reach many people but the trouble has been that he couldn't get the attention of the ones that he really wanted to get through to. And then there were others who really believed that Freddie was reaching out to them and he wasn't at all.

This is the next poem I received, which actually was a bit of a shock. I received it on 11 October 2001, not very long at all after my mother died.

Your mother has gone from your Earth,
But that is all.
Now she's happy and healthy,
And standing so tall.
Now she has met all us others,
And it makes sense at last,
That our life down on Earth,
Is not part of the past.
It's part of the whole thing,
Part of our love,
And she is still there beside you,
Although you think she's above.
But we don't go above you,
That story's not true.
We live right beside you,
Just stay close to you.

Chapter 9

On 16 December 2001 Norman and I went to see Keith for a reading. What basically came through that night were things from my mother. When my mother passed away, although she had had a hard life she had also had a good life. I didn't want her funeral to be morbid in any way. We had to follow the hearse for about twenty miles to the crematorium, so I had some really bright yellow roses with lots of trailing yellow ribbons on the coffin. This is one example of things I was told. The first thing she said was, "I saw the yellow roses and ribbons, they were lovely." At the time of my mother's death Keith was working away. He didn't even know my mother had died, so what she sent back was definitely proof in itself that we live on somehow. She also said, as I mentioned in Chapter 2, earlier in the book that she opened her eyes and her mother was there. She also said not to worry about her because she had also met her best friend Doris. She said she was really well and glad to get rid of that old body. She said everything we had talked about concerning Freddie was true. But also Freddie did come through saying he was glad that I was writing down all the things he was sending me, and he was hoping as I got more used to him that I would write a book.

That evening Keith invited Norman and I to his birthday party. It was on 12 January if I remember rightly, but definitely after the date that this poem came through to me, which was for Keith. I gave him this poem very reluctantly in case he thought, she has certainly got a wild imagination, and also because it was asking him if he would help Freddie and me, and really I thought this was rather cheeky, because it's a major undertaking. But Keith was happy about this poem and glad to help us. So here it is; see what you all think: Monday 7 January 2002.

Hi Keith it's me And I'm glad you can see,
That all along Mary's been telling the truth,
And I'm hoping it's you,
Who can bring us the proof.
I was lost when I left Earth,
Wasn't sure where to go.
But in the distance I saw
This wonderful glow.
So I slowly approached it,
And it made me secure.
It seemed warm and friendly,
I didn't want hurt any more.
So I stayed with the glow,
For a long time I'd say.
And I still stay close to it,
Even up to this day.
This glow you must know now,
Is Mary my friend.
And I'll stay close beside her,
Until it's the end,
Of her life on Earth.
Until she's back where she belongs,
And when she comes home,
She will be greeted with songs.
And there will be arms all around her,
She will receive so much love.
Because you don't know what we've seen,
From what you all call above.
So dear Keith please stay
And try to help us some way.

It needs to be told, this story of love.
I know it's hard because it's me.
But I want people to see
About how all of our world is just one.
About all of the hurts and the fun.
You know more than Mary
I've watched you, you see.

How to connect yourself to us,
To be really free.
So if you could help us some way,
Make her more wise,
Then boy will the world
Be in for a surprise.
She knows that I'm close,
But denies it a lot.
She can't really see
The special gift that she has got.
But I know that she trusts you,
She knows you don't lie.
So how great it would be,
Just to give it a try.

I'm sorry to use you,
Because I know your life's full.
But life can be busy.
And still feel quite dull.
So I promise you this Keith,
That once this has grown,
There are so many places,
That this story will be known.
We would have to be brave,
Never falter or waver,
And be strong and all stand in the light.
Because some people will scorn,
Make us feel tattered and torn.
And sometimes it will feel like a fight,
But a fight that's worth winning,
Because this is the beginning,
The beginning of something new,
But also for me, another chance
Just maybe Another chance, to prove I just grew
From a man down on
Earth Into what I'm now worth,
Because this way I live is the best,
And our life down on Earth is a test.

I am sure now that this had been planned by Freddie a long time ago, that he would somehow move Keith back into my life at the right time because, as the poem says, I have got complete faith in what this man says.

So we talked about this situation and we agreed to meet up at Keith's home, just the three of us, Norman, Keith and myself. Keith said he would try to bring Freddie through a bit closer than just messages. I said okay but I must admit I was a bit scared about all this. It was arranged for 6 March 2002, which was odd in itself because that is my granddaughter Jasmine's birthday. As the day approached I must admit I was wondering whether there was any way I could get out of it. I think that was because so many things had started building up where Freddie was concerned. I half expected to walk into Keith's flat and see Freddie sat on Keith's settee. That was a stupid thought, I know that now, but when you don't really understand these things your mind is bound to run a bit wild.

On the morning of 6 March 2002, this came through:

I know you are going to Keith's tonight,
But don't worry too much,
Just treat it all light.
I'll be there I promise,
And I'll make myself known.
There's no need for this upset,
Because you're not in it alone.
When I died Earthly,
I found in you a good friend.
So it will always make sense
That on you I depend.
Why are you scared?
I've known you ten years.
And I've always been there,
Through many troubles and tears.
So now this is exciting,
We've gone past that stage,
Tonight I will show you something,
That you couldn't ever know.

It's something that I always did,
Before I did a show.

But I was never actually told this. Does anyone know about something that Freddie always did before a show? This is where things start to get a bit deeper in this story, a little harder to take in. But I will try my best to explain as factually as I can.

We arrived at Keith's in the evening. He suggested that, if I wanted him to, he would go into a trance. I had heard about people going into trances, but had never witnessed anything that I could really take on board. But I did know what going into a trance means the medium opens up his soul and offers himself as an instrument to the spirit world, so that they can speak directly to us instead of sending messages. It isn't something to be messed around with though, you must know what you are doing, and I wouldn't recommend anyone having a go at this unless they were trained properly. This is how the evening went.

I was given a pen and writing pad, and was told that once things started coming through Keith I could write as much down as possible because Keith wouldn't be aware of anything that had been said while he was in trance. You might ask why he couldn't just have it taped like the readings. The reason is because there is so much energy gathered in the room on these occasions that it interferes with the sound on the tape. Also I must add that we have all got spirit guides with us, it seems, but when you become a medium then you gather extra guides around you to help you with the work you are doing. So we were all prepared. Keith went into his trance, and this is what came through.

Firstly someone spoke through Keith but obviously not Keith himself, if that makes any sense. He said:

I am one of this medium's spirit guides. I am glad to meet you. I would just like to say firstly that we know about your little grandson Jake. To us Jake is a beautiful energy and he wants me to say I love you grandma. It is his spirit that keeps him alive. He is growing spiritually all the time. He wants all the family to know that he loves them. We know there is no change in his body but he will not leave it until he is ready.

Then he, the spirit guide, told me that I had got my own mediumship through the Mercury Man, this is where the title of the book came from. The spirit guide said he would try to bring him through to me so that if I would like to I could converse with him. He said that while we were waiting for him he would tell me a few things He knew about this man. He said the Mercury Man wants to help the world he left behind. He said he was spiritually minded on Earth but never shared these thoughts with other people. He knew bad times when he was young but also as time went on knew what it was like to process everything. But he had to go through this process to achieve what he has become now.

And then suddenly Keith's voice changed and this very laboured breathing type of voice came through and I'm sure it was Freddie. He said:

When I was walking the Earth for the last month I could hardly breathe, but I was prepared to die. My memory of my life on Earth is very strong. I will communicate through you Mary if you will let me. I saw you sitting alone many years ago Mary. I know compassion is in your heart, I know the music and songs stirred you. I would like to work through you. I started writing a book but it was never completed. I don't know if that is true, I am just telling you what was told to me. I never really seemed to complete anything on Earth. I want to tell you about my life and my music. I always loved music. Even from a young age, I knew I would perform. It was my way of telling people how I felt. But I don't think they really understood me.

He said that people he had got to know since he passed over to the other side were helping him also to learn how to come through directly to me. He said that he originates from a very ancient and old order. (I don't understand what this means but I am including it because this is what was said to me.) He said that he once lived in a time where order didn't exist, and that he knew this because when we get back to the spirit world everything is made known to us about any past lives. He explained that he was just experimenting to see how good he could do this communicating and that he would say a lot more another time. He said that we had met in our dreams. We had met; I had had many, many dreams about Freddie. He continued: "I have watched you all along your life from when I first found you. I have chosen you for this job in hand. The book. You are right for me. I have been with you all along helping you write all your information down." He explained that he couldn't stay long but he wished me well and love, and also wished Norman well and love.

Then someone else spoke, I don't know who, saying, "We are all talking together over here about your book, we are all excited and trying to help you. That's what Freddie wants, his own feelings were very explicit." Then I was asked if I would like to ask a question. Actually what was said to me was, "You don't say much, don't you want to ask me some questions?" So I asked, "Why has Freddie chosen me?" The answer was:

> *Because you are an emotional person, quite passionate. You are Freddie's vessel, he has chosen you because you have got an open mind. He has chosen you just because he can express what he is feeling through you. But you must be patient; it has taken over ten years to get you to absorb all this. But don't question any more. Just accept and trust Freddie now. He will guide you through it. You worry too much. You don't have to write this book but we all know your heart wants to do it. We don't want you to have to stand up and tell this story, but put yourself forward to write all these things down. You are Freddie's instrument. This book won't be about his life in music. It will be about what he was. People didn't understand him. Some of the things he tells you maybe won't make sense to you but just be patient.*

This spirit then said he needed to go. Then someone else, another voice, spoke and said, "Greetings, my friends. We have now opened your minds to us. We thank you for your love and attention. Please convey our love and thanks to him, your medium. We will all meet again, but the medium needs to rest now."

After this was over I was also absolutely amazed can the spirit world get that close that they can actually talk to you? Yes, they obviously can, if they find the right person, but I had never witnessed anything like this before. Up until now I had only really had messages and of course the poems coming through to me, so this experience was completely different, much more intense and personal.

A few days later another poem came through, and I must stress that these poems that I get come through to me really fast; I can hardly keep up with writing them. It's not until I read them back to myself afterwards that I see that they make sense, but if I try to sit down to write a poem nothing at all will come through. This is very frustrating, but I suppose it does prove that they are sent to me.

I am dating everything as best I can, so that you can all see how things follow on from one another.

Monday 11 March 2002.

Everything that's going on,
And whirling through your mind.
And always seems to come to you,
In some kind of rhyme,
Will pass in time,
Just wait and see,
And we'll talk together
You and me.
We've rode our way,
Through the hard part,
And now you do believe,
I've spoken through our friend,
And now I know It's something you can perceive.

I know you're so excited,
Well I can tell you so am I.
I've waited so long for this time.
Now we can really reach the sky.
I can't wait to tell you my story,
I can't wait to get it all done.
But you wait and see,
Things that I bring you
Will be lots and lots of fun.
I'm really glad I found you, dear,
I'm really glad you care.
I'm sure all of us together,
Will make people so aware,
That life goes on forever,
Not just our time on Earth.
In the end it comes together,
And then we see what it is worth.
So go and tell your friend, dear Norman,
That I've sent you through this rhyme.
And he will need to be strong and stand by you,
For things to come out In our time.

Monday March 18 2002.

Why don't you write your book?
Why don't you take a closer look?
Why don't you lift the veil,
And see what lays inside?
And then your hurts,
They may start to subside.
You know I really care,
You know I'm always there.
And I know it's hard,
Because things seem to be going so wrong.
You two will win in the end,
You'll see my friend
And you'll laugh and you'll say,
Now look who's tall and strong.

And you'll start to see why,
Things seem to have gone so wrong.
This is your turning point,
So listen out for my song.
My song will be so great,
And you'll know it's more than fate.
It will be a story of love,
A tale so old,
A tale that's strong and bold,
And needs to be told.
It's a tale of you and me,
That no one else can see.

So in this last poem, there is the comment on the song again, and yet, try as I might, I cannot pick up on anything that relates in any way to a song. Maybe someone will be able to help me on that one in the future.

I must say that at this time I was full of hurt, partly due to the fact that I missed my mother so much and partly my marriage breaking down. Also at this time I was living with Norman and his family so there were many, many stresses for all of us. So how I even received these poems I really don't know. Freddie Mercury must have a very determined character. But I do also believe now, looking back on all of this, that he was trying so hard just to prove to me he was still around me. Why I have been as privileged as this I really will never know.

More poems did come through to me before this next one,

but they are very personal, and besides, I would never fit them all into the book. So I am trying to pick out the most relevant ones. I really don't know what to make of this one. It sounds as though my mother sent it, but I can't really see how my mother could put this poem together. But here goes:

Saturday 20 April 2002

Hello my Mary it's me.
And I'm coming to you with such glee,
And if it wasn't for dear Freddie Mercury

This would never be able to be.
He has taught me how to reach you,
Has become my very best friend,
And the things that you told me about him,
You will find they are true in the end.

I know that you're hurting about me,
But I'm fine really fine.
Never fear.
And the life that we shared close together
I will always hold close, very dear.

I know that it's hard that you break
From this pattern.
I know you're trying to hold on to the past,
But it isn't like that,
And the life that we lived,
It isn't just part of the past.
It's part of the all,
Part of now.
And I wish I could show you how,
We are all so involved with each other,
But I love you like there's no other.

And to me you are like my turtle dove,
Because a turtle dove to me,
Is the other half you see.
Is the other half of the time that we spent,
Wrapped in love and the joy that it sent.
We were mother and child,
And that's putting it mild,
You were my saviour,
My very best friend,
But Freddie says,
I'll now have to end.

So look to the future,
Be brave and be strong.

Don't live your life thinking,
You did me such wrong.
So good night my dear girl,
I still love you.
And Freddie says, tell her I do too.
Mum
X

My mother always had a thing about turtle doves. She couldn't stand to see one on its own, because she said they always paired up for life, and if she saw one on its own that was sad for her because she said it would now have to live the rest of its life alone. And if it wasn't for my being there for her through her life she would, I am sure, have felt very alone. So this poem really does make sense.

I would say from the date of this last poem, that life became almost intolerable for all of us in Norman's house until we finally did leave there on 2 August 2002.

Chapter 10

The house didn't seem to be selling as quickly as expected, and we were all, by this time, getting very agitated. So I must just add this small story because it is a twist in the tale really.

I was thinking about all sorts of things I suppose, remembering the past, wondering why life seemed to be becoming more and more of a mess. And I remember thinking, Mike used to say if you pray to the Lord sincerely he will help you. So that night, which was Wednesday 8 May 2002, I did pray to the Lord and asked him, please can you persuade someone to buy this house of Norman's so that we can all move on and have a new start.

On the 9 May 2002 some people came to look at the house and said they would like to buy it. I didn't think they ever would though; it was too much of a coincidence, because the house had been on the market for quite a long time and they were the first family with any deep interest. But amazingly they did buy it. So it seems like my prayers were answered. Also they have got a son named Freddie, which to me is another strange twist, and I quite like the idea of their living there, enjoying their life, and their little son Freddie growing up there.

Of course in between May and August it was a hard waiting game because the buyers could change their minds. But 11 May one of Freddie's pictures fell off the wall for no apparent reason. This led me to thinking that, just for something to do, I would try to send a poem to Freddie the way that he sent them to me, just to see if he could pick up on them the way that I could. This is what I wrote, and as you can see it is very short:

For God's sake Freddie,
Please send me a poem.

Things are coming to a head,
And my frustration's growing.
So can't you please help me,
Give us a sign,
Show me the future,
That's Norman's and mine.

I didn't expect anything back but the next day this came back:

How much do you want?
I knocked off your picture.
And now maybe you've started
To look into the scripture.
There is a God you know,
And he loves you so.
And Mike knew you didn't really believe
But wasn't hurt although you had agreed.
But Mike was right in all the things he told you.
That God exists,
And he'll be there to hold you.
He will hold you when you're down,
Make you better, make you good.
But he doesn't wear a crown,
Or regalia, as we would.
He is just a simple being,
And he wants us to be seeing,
That if we ask for help, he'll be right there,
And because he suffered on Earth
He doesn't care.
That's over and it's done,
But still he is the one,
Who proved a point, and helped us
Open our eyes.

So I'm glad you prayed to Him,
Although it took a while.
But maybe now you'll live your life
With style.

You and Norman are good people,
And you have both been climbing a steeple.
But now you're nearly there,
And you'll both be able to fly.
So don't fret too much dear,
Because you know I am always near.
And Mike is saying he's glad you're in at last.
And now you know the truth,
Hold on real fast.

This poem did actually make me feel guilty. Had I expected Mike to believe in Freddie but had never really took anything on board about the Lord? I think that's possible. I think at the time all I wanted was to make Mike feel safe and Freddie was that safety, because if I could just make him see that if Freddie was free so could he be. And although I listened to everything Mike had to say maybe I didn't take it all on board that much. But I certainly have now. And here is another lesson to be learned. Don't just take it for granted that people won't know these things when they get to the other side, because they will.

Between May and August 2002 life was just swallowed up really. I had no time to think about this Freddie thing. I was still grieving for my mother, I would say, because we had always been so close. A great big chunk of my life had been ripped away. I was going through a divorce, not knowing where our future lay, really not knowing where we were going to end up living when Norman's house was sold. And then there was Jake, of course, who was always there in my mind anyway. His life wasn't keeping on an even keel; sometimes he had spells of being very unwell.

But strangely enough, over this stretch of time, I still received about fifteen poems, all very personal, like someone, or something was trying to let me know they were still there. Was it my subconscious, you could ask? No, it definitely wasn't. They were definitely being filtered through to me from somewhere.

Eventually everything sorted itself out as it usually does. I was, at the time, hoping and praying that I would get my home back through my divorce. My divorce was over, we had moved from Norman's, and we ended up living in my original home, but that's another story. But I will add to this story just the end of one personal poem and the following one:

18 July 2002

So look forward now, dear,
We are happy for you.
I'm sure you know who this is,
But I will give you a clue,
I've known you more than ten years.
You're very special to me,
And I heard you say earlier,
That you hoped I could see.
Well of course I can see you,
I watch you both everyday
And I'll be glad when you're happy.
But I just want to say,
Please don't forget me when your life is on track,
Sometimes sit quietly, and try to look back.
At the things we have shared,
And the times we have cared.

On Tuesday 23 July 2002, I found out I could have my old house back. This is what came through that evening after I had got over the excitement:

And so the day has come,
My caring lovely one.
Your rewards are here at last,
You're on your way,
And we are all here,
And we all just want to say,
Well done our dearest friend.
We are so glad you won in the end,
And the future will be so good,
Just wait and see.
And I'm sorry I thought you might start to forget me.
I saw you there today,

Kissing my photo right away.
And I know I was such a fool,
To ever doubt you.
But the truth is
I don't want to be without you.
Because this closeness we have got,
Well that really says the lot.
I'm dead they think,
And you are still alive,
So how the hell they think,
Can a bond like this survive?
But this is what we should do,
Together me and you.
Prove to everybody, that we are all just as one.
And we can link up together,
With people we think are gone.

There are two reasons why I have included these poems. Firstly, I did take Freddie's photo off the wall and kiss it when I found out about the house, and secondly, and much more importantly, I have never heard Freddie say that someone met him when he passed over. I do hope they did and he just hasn't told me. But if they didn't I just want him to know that I do care.

So by now I was starting to feel a bit better about the loss of my mother. But of course having this belief does help. Now all this bad time was starting slowly to move behind us, in early October 2002 I did hear this from Freddie:

> *If you had written this book for me years ago I wouldn't have so much to tell you, because it takes time to adjust and learn how to connect and gain information. We seem, or at least I did, to go through stages. Firstly we are held to the Earth to some extent by our emotions. We spend time wanting to let our closest ones on Earth know that we are all right. This is frustrating because we choose how hard we try from here, not really anyone realizes some people may just wonder, but that's about as far as it gets. So we in the first stages of our moving*

over see people crying over us and of course that hurts us as well and it is very hard to cope with the fact that we can't reach them. But time as you see it changes these things and although we remain who you remember and will always be that, we also start to open ourselves up to the fact that we are more that we were on Earth. This will be hard for some people, who read this book, to digest, I realize that. But this is the way that it is here. But it doesn't mean that the love we feel for certain people on the Earth plane fades. Look at how I have never moved away from you Mary. So in a way this should prove what I am saying to the people about this. It's just that we grow more in ourselves as our time goes on in spirit. We will always be learning though, going through different stages of learning. We are not superior to people on Earth, when we go to spirit, I wouldn't want people to believe that.

Chapter 11

Norman and I made arrangements with Keith Hall that when he had some free time we would get together and try to bring Freddie through again. I wasn't so scared this time now that I had already witnessed what happens. So we arranged to meet on 18 October 2002, which, strangely enough, was five years to the day since Jake fell into the canal. It was just that that was when Keith had some free time. So we all met at his flat. This time we had a tape running. Although there is a lot of interference on the tape, at least I've still got it. I have spent hours listening to small sections of the tape at a time, writing the content down and then doing a bit more. What follows is now what it contains, although Norman and I, of course also witnessed all this in person.

Keith went into a trance for me and for the spirits of course. Firstly his main spirit guide came through. I won't tell you his name because that is personal. He introduced himself to us, and said it was very nice to meet us. But you must remember, as you read this account, you can't see these spirits you can only hear them. He said:

> *I am what you would term the doorkeeper of the mind of the medium; I am talking with you about the purpose of our sitting here tonight. Our true purpose is to understand how the young lady will be able to open her mind and allow the spirit world to work through her. Here tonight I have a man who wishes to converse with this lady. He says he was involved in the music world on Earth, and it seems that in this spirit world they call him the Mercury Man. You must understand that just because I am the medium's doorkeeper between the*

two worlds I don't automatically know every spirit that exists here. They come to me to help them to reach you so I don't know this man and I will be learning with you. He is telling me he has been in the spirit world a number of years now and he really does want to communicate with the Earth from his spirit home. He tells me he was somewhat of a celebrity on Earth through his music and songs so please bear with me; I have to learn and understand all this also. As I talk to you at this moment in time, others are preparing his mind to work through this instrument Keith. He wants you to understand in his own words what he wishes from the young lady, and the connection that is between him and her. This man has tried many times to come through to people on the Earth plane, partly because of certain remorses of his life here on Earth, and the pleasures he gained from his popularity and the monitory gains he created here on Earth. All different things are happening here for the preparation of bringing this man through so he can be close to you and say what he wishes. So don't worry about the strange noises that you are hearing. They are created from the atmosphere and the energies building up in the room. So be prepared for anything because this man is having problems in coping with the different vibration on the Earth. But don't worry we will try very hard to get him through for you.

The noises mentioned were Keith's video recorder which kept running on and going off. The tape player was making a droning noise, nothing frightening. The spirit guide continued:

Before we attempt to bring the communication through the Mercury Man, I want the young lady to understand she has the power within her to be able to work through her mind. We want to encourage her to write her book. It is her that he has chosen not this instrument I am using now. This Mercury Man, they are telling me from the Spirits, is very aware of her presence. He is aware of her thoughts and he invades her mind day and night. Very little time does she have when she doesn't think of this man. He has chosen her because she has a receptive mind. She has a raw mind, not preconditioned by spirit. They are telling me that he had a lot of celebrity status when he was on the Earth plane. But he doesn't particularly require that celebrity status now. He is saying that he wishes to make amends for some of the things that he could have done on the Earth and didn't. He wants to purvey the feeling of love to everyone. He is saying that he is a man that loved life and his music and songs. He has tried to work in different ways through many people on Earth, trying to give them ideas, trying to spur them on. He is saying at this moment in time there is a kind of book being put together but all it talks about is his life and his ego and eccentricities. All the things he now regrets, since he has been in the spirit world. He would just like to put the record straight on that. But he likes the raw mind the young lady possesses and is hoping to work through her. He is saying all this came about many years ago, this affection and communication between the lady and this man. He is saying that when he was on Earth he was often very theatrical but he had a good sense of humour. He laughs even at what we are doing right at this moment. If people had talked to him about this subject on the Earth plane, he would not have really understood it. He would have listened and been interested but not understood all this, although he is saying he did have his own thoughts about all this but kept them to himself. What I am doing right at this moment is preparing the way for this man. I am not sure if this man will be able to use the mind of this medium or not. So I will go for a while, see if we can prepare him. In the meantime I am in control now of his mind. I have his mind here with me. Mind that's what we all are mind, or call it the Spirit.

Then there was a long pause; we all just sat quietly in the room. Keith was still in trance. Then suddenly someone, Freddie I am sure, started speaking. He said:

> *I have only been able to come through to you Mary through your dreams and through your mind. This is a wonderful opportunity to say hello. I seem to have so much to say, so many things that I wish to give back to the Earth. I've still got my sense of humour and I still like a laugh and a joke. I do want you to write that book, Mary. Many years ago now, when I first recognized that I could reach your mind I knew you were the person who I had to work through. There is a need for some peace on this Earth. Let us talk and write of the peace that is needed on this Earth. Until I changed my body, the body of light that I am now, I didn't realize that we all carry the same truths in the end. I only understood before this what could be possible for one person and I used this for my music and writing. But looking back it all seemed to be about monetary gain, about the ego, about who I was, not the real message. I did try within my songs, especially the later songs. Most of the music and words I recognized came from a source outside myself. Now I know where that source comes from. Music, words, melodies, fears, where they come from. Nothing on this Earth produces it. It comes from spirit. For the book there will be others who will come through to prepare you to open your mind and allow you to work exactly as we are doing at this moment. Recording it and telling the truth. It will not be a book of my fame and my fortunes. Hopefully it will help to show people a better way forward. There is a starved world out there. What I have learned about the spirit world is that I seem to have to die to learn the truth about many things. I ask you to write this book in the simplest of ways, not cleaver not with any antidotes. Because of my name they will listen. The Mercury Man, I like that, but that's ego, but I would like that title. Hopefully it will be about the future, about changes in oneself, the nation*

and the world. We are standing now on the edge of a very frightening time. I lived through one myself the Cold War and the A-bomb. So let's talk about our lives on Earth. I lived a reckless life. Because of it I used to say if a bomb drops on us, so what, don't worry about it. If there was something that was a threat in my life I would just say, so what, that was my attitude. I loved life and took the consequences of that love, so what, I lost my sense of responsibility especially in my younger years. The first thing I realized when I passed to the spirit world was I could have done so much more. There are many in my profession on the Earth plane now who do great works; turn fame and fortune into always helping the world. I feel I did not do my share. I should have done but don't let the world think that I am sad, because I am not. I did on Earth everything that I wanted to do, but my way, sometimes without any cares of the consequences. I am told that I weighed my own life up, judged myself, but in doing that I created music. I was an instrument on Earth for this reason. Just as this man at the moment is an instrument for me to be able to talk to you and I thank him kindly. I have no regrets for myself but I had to die to know that I should have done so much more. One thing I have found about this wonderful truth it's not on a religious level not a dogmatic level, it's really and truly a way of life that touches everyone's life. I met on the Earth plane the man called John Lennon. We have also met up here in the spirit world. It sounds like a lot of stars in the sky doesn't it, and yet I am here in this room with you at the moment in your very atmosphere. The atmosphere of this earthly world is very heavy; it makes it harder to express yourself. It's strange but being here with you I almost feel human again, it's the sensation of being drawn back so close to, actually on the Earth I suppose. There is a collection of minds in the spirit world that I have joined with; they will all try to help you with this book but you will have to listen to what they say when they draw close to you. The strangest feeling that I have right now is that I would like to smoke; I am very aware of wanting to smoke. I used to love a cigarette. The name Freddie Mercury talking about a cigarette, there is your first joke. I know you find it awesome that you have been chosen for this; Mary don't be. You have the enthusiasm and you even have the feeling that you want to do it, this work. I have worked hard to make you hear me. I will find a way of working with you Mary. I will find a way of getting my thoughts into your mind. To do that you need to clear your own mind, dedicate yourself to so much time a day whatever you can afford in your life allowing me to come through you I will dictate what I wish to be written down. It is complicated because your mind can easily interfere with what I am trying to say. It is quite emotional for me to talk like this to someone who I have been linking with on the Earth plane, actually talking to you. I'm trying all the time to communicate with you, Mary. Allow our minds to blend one with one. If we allow ourselves to become almost as one it will help you to understand that everything that gets written down will be coming through you not from you. When you start this story start from the beginning, from when I first came into your mind, that this man, myself, was around you. Tell them about the disbelief that I was around you. The story will start to unfold. You won't do it overnight, you won't do it in months. Just let it manifest through you. I am told that I must go now, but before I go I wish to thank you for allowing me to come into your mind. Thank you for accepting and believing in me. Already the true friendship has now begun. God bless you my love.

Then someone else spoke through Keith and said, "My name is Ching Ling. I believe this lady has felt my presence with her before." I replied, "No I can't say I have really", which I must say I was quite embarrassed about, but he just said:

Never mind, you will as time goes on. I am one of your group of guides that has been allowed to come through to try to teach you a little bit about how to prepare your mind for the task ahead of you. You need to sit. I'm here to teach you how to sit, and prepare your mind; the spirit world wants to come through you. If you allow yourself to relax, to breathe very deeply, to prepare your mind; don't ask questions of it or form any opinions or else what we are trying to achieve might not happen. You are an instrument to be used by the spirit world. If you can accept this truth you can be a good instrument. It will need practice, it takes a while to allow your mind to go away from your body for a while. If you keep practising you will do it. I am just one of your helpers who comes close to you. There will be more than one.

A very faint "Listen" then came from somewhere in the room. Then this spirit, Ching Ling, said:

The instrument that we have been using, Keith, has pledged his help to you. He has pledged it all his knowledge and to help you achieve your aim. I must now go. We have been working through this instrument and his mind long enough. We will bring him back to conscious mind now. But before I go I say God bless you all and thank you for being there for us and listening to us. There are many questions on the lips of the lady I can see. The instrument is coming back to consciousness now. He will explain things to her.

So now Keith was back out of his trance and we just sat and talked. I told him I had heard a very faint "Listen" in the room but he said there was nothing to worry about. Because the spirit world had drawn so close to us, I had picked that up on my own. Then he said he could also hear someone very gently calling Mary, and asked whether I could hear that, but I couldn't.

Chapter 12

So for the next few days I did try very hard to relax and prepare my mind to give Freddie a chance to come through and say things if he really wanted to that badly. For a few days there was nothing, but I always kept a pen and writing pad with me just in case. And then out of the blue it all started coming through. But I must tell you a little story before I start. My family, Keith and I have all said that Norman doesn't really look like a Norman, that a different name would suit him better but this was just between ourselves. Now I am going to tell you all what has came directly though to me from Freddie. I am going to relate it in this book in the order I received it, so if the story doesn't seem to run smoothly that is because of the order in which I was told this information. It's a bit like a journal really.

Wednesday 23rd October 2002.

Norman had gone somewhere so I was sat on my own, which was unusual because Norman and I are usually together or were at this time. Out of the blue I heard someone say, in my mind:

> *Let's have a little talk together while Norman is out of the way. Norman, you're right it doesn't suit him. Let's call him Tutti Frutti, how about that? It will just be between us, something special, let's see what it brings. I know this is all very strange for you. We have mingled for a very long time now but not to this extent. For a while until you get used to all this connecting up I want you to see me in your mind's eye as Freddie Mercury because I know you love this Freddie Mercury. So this will bond us closer together to get this book together. I have never in all my*

time on Earth or in the spirit world seen anyone being so adamant about not having anything bad said against this Freddie Mercury. It doesn't seem to matter what has come into your life since I went to spirit and entered your life, it has never made you move away from me and I will carry that forever. Oh, I know when your terrible tragedy arrived in your family's lives it was like nothing else mattered but I was still there with you and I know it seemed forever to you but see it through my eyes: your little grandson had his accident in October 1997 but by February 1998 Peter was in Torquay and once you heard he was there that had your mind ticking again. Time doesn't really mean much to us in the spirit world but we can relate to it, if we need to. And as time goes on and you get used to this situation you will come to see that Freddie Mercury was what I was meant to be on Earth not who I am, but don't let go of your love of the man because of this because that is very special; hold to that always. When we eventually meet in the spirit world there will be no room for anyone else for a short while. That sounds selfish to other earthly people, I know, but it will make sense in the end. It will be like two complete strangers meeting although the bond is already there. Our connection is from the two worlds, which really are one. Don't ever be afraid of all this though, because when we first meet you will recognize me as the Freddie Mercury. I will now try to explain to you that there are not so many spirits that people believe. Don't get this wrong though, we are all spirits and we are all important, and when we leave the Earth we all go home to our real place. But once I heard you say that being reincarnated must be a bit like being recycled. I found that quite amusing at the time, but actually that is very much as it is. There are a mass of spirits who just seem to go round in circles; they come to the Earth, don't learn anything, come back home, get sent again, still don't learn anything, and so it goes on. And then there are others who come to the Earth more than once because they chose to, to learn, and then the time will come when they will choose not to visit the Earth again because they will have learned all their earthly needs. And then there are others like you or many others, Keith, myself for instance, who won't go back to the Earth plane. We will work from here. For now I will say so long. Just take this all in. We will talk again soon. We will have to find a better way of controlling Tutti Frutti so that we can have time together.

Poor Norman. I think Freddie must try to control him to a certain degree because the next morning he got up and said, "I think I'll spend today fixing the shed roof ", which meant I had the day to myself. Instantly, as soon as I was on my own, there was Freddie again.

Thursday 24 October 2002.

Let's have another talk, shall we, while Tutti Frutti is busy. I remember very clearly the first time I entered into your life. I passed over on the 24 November and I entered your life on 25. I was drifting, already getting used to my new surroundings but also desperate that someone would know that I still existed. Part of me saw a vision of a nice lady looking completely bewildered and shocked that she was hearing on the television that this Freddie Mercury had died. Who's Freddie Mercury, I could see her thinking, but as they flashed up a picture of me on the screen I knew this lady had seen something more than earthly things. You were that lady. It was so obvious to me that you didn't seem to know me and yet you recognized my picture and I could see instantly that your heart went out to me, and from that moment I knew I must contact you somehow. 24 November, I will forever remember that date. The day Freddie Mercury left the Earth. I can still remember what the sensation of dying was like. My first memory is of being lifted out of my body, gently, by unseen hands. Everything seemed like slow motion. Imagine how you feel when you are slightly drunk and everything slows down in a way but you are still very aware of things. This is the closest I can explain to all of you of what it felt like. Then everything seemed to speed up and I was moving fast away from my body. I seemed to turn completely around and face myself. I saw this empty shell of a body that was lying on the bed. It looked old and worn out, not like me at all. I remember being shocked at the sight of it. Then it dawned on me that I myself was all right, I was alive and free again, I didn't need that body, it had just been loaned to me to carry me about on Earth. I didn't instantly know when I arrived in spirit that I was not really Freddie Mercury; I still thought I was for a long time. It is only as time went on and I started to learn more that I saw that this person on Earth who became Freddie Mercury for a while was only part of what I really am. That will be very hard for earthly people to take in, I know, but believe me we are all more than what is sent to Earth. People still gather round my house, you know, and I am long gone from there. My house, that sounds strange now, but I loved that house; it was my security, my sanctuary for my last years on Earth. Before that house I never really had what you could call complete security. Although as I look back I don't think I even wanted it then, but I did love that house. I still go and visit now and again but it isn't a need any more, it's more like a thought.

That seemed to be the end of the talking and then this small poem came through:

At last this is coming together,
We are finally sorting this out.
We are starting now to unravel this thing,
I hope there's some who can figure this out.
I hope that it opens their eyes to life,
I hope that it gives them some peace.
That our life doesn't just come to an end,
On our death.

I hope that will bring some release,
To people who are dreading what is coming to them,
To people who are full of fear.
I want them to see, there's no need to be scared.
I want them to know we are near.

Chapter 13

I didn't receive anything again until 4 November 2002. This is what came through:

> *As I lay in my bed for hours and hours at a time as my illness progressed, waiting for death in a way, trying to come to terms with things and the way they had turned out, one thing I hoped against hope for was that I would live on after my life on Earth. I didn't know if this was really possible; I didn't know how it would be if I did survive. But as I remember all about that time now, something deep inside of myself would never let go of this hope. I never discussed it with anyone. I was afraid of being laughed at. You see, my dear, you are not the only one afraid of being laughed at. Life became unbearable for my last few months on Earth. I am not telling you this for sympathy, because I am fine and happy. I am just stating a fact that however unbearable life becomes on Earth we do step out of that situation when we pass into spirit. But I need to point out when we pass over by natural means not helping ourselves on the way at all, that is a completely different situation and should never ever be considered. When I first came to realize that I had survived, I wanted to comfort all the people who were crying around my body; that I was fine look I'm fine, that body means nothing anymore. But it slowly dawned on me that they just couldn't see at all that I still existed. To all of them Freddie Mercury was dead and gone and they would have to find a way to come to terms with that. I must stress the fact that it is very frustrating to watch all*

this. The last thing you want is for your loved ones to be hurt, but of course the other side of me and the character that survived with me wanted to be off, away from this sad situation. I had been given another chance and I didn't want to waste it. To get rid of that worn out body was wonderful, to feel so free was wonderful. To try to explain this to you all is very complicated because this is how I was feeling about the people I had left behind on my death. Some other people, I have come to learn with time, when they die and leave their bodies, and come back to spirit. They never ever bother with the Earth plane again. They feel they had their time there and there is no reason at all to try to communicate with anyone on the Earth plane. They will meet up with their families and friends when they themselves pass over. But in the meantime there will not be any communication. Then there are others of us who would desperately love to let their loved ones know that they are fine, and never get heard. This is sad because it is only because a lot of people on Earth are afraid to believe all this, afraid of being ridiculed, and so through these fears miss out on this wonderful thing. I myself seemed, in the first stages of my being in spirit to have and still have this deep feeling of letting people know that we do survive death. I was lucky I found you and it seems many years to you for everything that has happened to the time that has come to write this book. But we needed that time, to gain the trust, to make you believe. For it to be seen through this book that true love, when it is found, wherever it comes from, never dies, no matter what else comes into a person's life. I must be truthful with you though, Mary, there was another reason why I held on to you in the first stages of all this. It was so very obvious that something deep inside you was holding you tight to this situation of Freddie Mercury dying. And as I was drifting backwards and forwards because this was all very new and strange to me, remember so I would drift quite often back to my own earthly home and found these visits very upsetting. Many times I had laid in my bed in the later stages of my life at least comforted by the fact that what I considered my family around me through these times would, at least, have each other when I passed away and they could support each other. But that wasn't happening from what I could see. I had had promises made to me and they were not being carried out now that I had gone, and at this time this hurt so bad, I didn't want this to happen. I didn't want to see this, because our emotions stay strongly with us when we pass over into spirit. I was very disappointed and very hurt. But you, this complete stranger, obviously cared very much and had never gained anything from me, ever, in any way. So it made me cling to you more in a way, but I realize now myself that it helped the bond between us to become stronger.

This next section is obviously Freddie speaking directly to all of you. It came through about 15 November 2002.

Hello at last all you lovely people. I have waited so long for this chance to be able to reach you all in this way. To let you know that we do live on after what is called death on Earth. This is very unusual for a spirit to be able to come through as clear as this. Usually I realize we consider ourselves extremely lucky to be able to pass on short messages to our friends and loved ones on Earth. So I feel very privileged, but as you can see it has taken many years for me to achieve this and if it wasn't for this dear lady this would never have been able to be, so please do not ridicule her. She has done this very reluctantly, I know this. In a way I have controlled her into all this by staying in her mind for all these years but we are also friends and we will remain friends. I know there are not many of you who will be able to understand this at all, but it is possible for someone from the spirit world to reach out to someone on the earth plane. And often it is easier if we reach out to a person who is a stranger to us on Earth because their mind is more clear to what we are trying to say, not cluttered up with memories of us. It has only become possible to talk to you all as easily as this with the help of many friends and advisers in the spirit world and spiritually minded people on the Earth plane. Especially our good friend Keith who has very kindly and very willingly opened his mind to us all. How can I ever thank him? The biggest problem this lady will have to face when this book is released is she will be bombarded with people asking, how do you do that, talk to Freddie Mercury, and some of them will try to ridicule her. But she must just calmly say, I listened and I learned and it took me a very long time to even start to understand all this. And maybe if you people who prefer to ridicule me would open your minds perhaps you would be able to understand this a bit better and pick up on these things yourselves. Who knows, you might be able to help someone out there as this lady has helped me. There's something I need to tell this lady now. When she went to Peter for me I know she thought it was just all for him. It wasn't, it was for her as well. How could she ever deny to herself again that this was me. Some people, friends of mine, I know have felt my presence around them, still do. This is simply because I am often with them. But of course part of them feels this is a bit spooky, not quite right. One of my biggest hopes through your reading this book is that somehow I can at least make some of you see that there is nothing spooky or strange. It is just a natural process in our lives and of course we, spirits, as you think of us, will come close to the ones we loved and cared for on Earth. Not to scare you, not to interfere with your lives, just to be close to you sometimes, see how you are getting on, because we care. We are just as real as you people, just living on another vibration, which makes it not possible for you to see us, but you can often sense our presence. Sadly most people disregard these feelings as nothing but just imagination and lose the chance of experiencing this wonderful thing. I would say, looking back on my life as a child, my growing up years on Earth, I was not really contented. I was always looking for something different, always wondering why I was different, always wondering also why I was to a certain degree disregarded, at least in my mind, at such a young age. I know now, as the years went by, this spurred me on, made something grow stronger in my mind, made me believe that one day I would be somebody, I would be noticed. But if you people look at life in general you will come to realize that many remembered names on Earth had, what shall we say, quite empty childhoods. When you come home to the spirit world, because that is what this is where I am now, home, you then realize that your young years on Earth had to be like this because it is that that spurs you on to be someone noticed, make a mark. I hope my becoming someone has helped many people in different ways because that helps now to make me happy and content and I do hope I can help some of you a lot more yet. If I can do this it will help fulfil all the things I should have done in my time on Earth. I am sure some people will say to this lady, why didn't Freddie Mercury choose one of his true fans to communicate through instead of a person who had no interest is him at all? So I will answer this for you. I didn't really choose this lady for anything at all in the first place, she was just there when I needed someone. To find her was just as big a shock to me as it was for her that I had arrived in her life, and anyway, I am not looking for glory, this time. I am just glad of my name from the past because when you recognize that this is me I am hoping it will get you all to take notice of what I am trying to portray to you. Because, you see, if I can live on like this and be able to reach out and tell you, then how can anyone just die for good, through their death on Earth? I wasn't given any privileges here in the spirit world just because I was Freddie Mercury. We are all spirits, we are all equal and we do all live on.

The next thing I received after this was another poem on 18 November 2002:

This is a story that needs to be told,
It reaches through two worlds
And is powerful and bold.
Powerful for me,
Bold on the lady's part,
But people must see,
This comes straight from her heart.
I've gained the power,
She's gained the right.
So now let's begin, let it shine in the light.
Pass on to other people,
Things are never just lost.
It's just a trial time on Earth
And we just seem to pay the cost.

But the better we live,
While we are going through this time,
And the kinder we are,
Makes our passing much more fine.
We will be greeted by friends
And so will know where we are going.

So we need to open up our hearts,
And let our soul start growing.
So read this book my friends,
And see this isn't where it ends,
Our lives are eternal,
They go on forever.
I hope you all learn some things from this.
I hope it gives your life more bliss
And takes away the hurt of losing someone.
I'll be the proof and say,
See we are not gone.
Just removed from out of sight,
Waiting for you in the light.

On 24 November 2002 I sat quietly for a while giving Freddie a chance to come close if he would like to. I actually didn't expect anything at all because I still feel now, even after all that I have written, that it's amazing that anyone at all from the spirit world can draw as close to a person on Earth as this and give all this information, let alone Freddie Mercury, and because it was the anniversary of his death I was sure he would want to draw close to more important people that me. But I did hear this:

> *I am here with you and I do know what today is and it is nice to know that people still care. But really I have moved away from all that. This time now is much more important. That time was really just part of this time. To me it is much more important that we get this book together.*

Chapter 14

On 8 December 2002 I met a gypsy lady by sheer coincidence. It was at a street fair that I went to and she persuaded me into her caravan, as they do. I told her I didn't have a lot of interest in fortune telling. I was more interested in the spiritual side of life. But she said, "I won't be telling your fortune, I will tell you about your complete life from the day you were born until the present day. If I don't tell you the truth don't pay me." But she did tell me the complete truth about my life over the years, everything that had happened to me and my daughters; I was amazed. But one thing she did say was I had got a man from the spirit world who had black hair she said she could see this black hair distinctly and who was always by my side; always there for me. She said it was my father, which I must say I actually didn't like hearing, because if he didn't want me or my mother while he was down on Earth, in my eyes he needn't bother now. But I do know that my father didn't have black hair. I didn't tell the gypsy lady this though. I didn't really want to talk about it. I did for the next few days find it quite upsetting that there was a possibility that my father was around me.

So a few days later I sat quietly trying to meditate, thinking, well if Freddie can talk to me then if this is my father around me maybe he would like to come through and talk to me. It will give him a chance to do a bit of explaining. But, instead, this is what I heard, or these thoughts were put into my head:

> *Your father's not here, it's Freddie. The gypsy woman will try to convince you this isn't me, but she will be wrong. They just don't like things like this. I have watched you since you went to her, and she told you things right. She*

knows what she is doing, to a level, a very good level, and it would even be good for you to see her again. But they disregard the spirit world the way you see it. They do believe, but only in their own way and their mind won't stretch as far as me. She may even see me, but she will tell you it's false. I know you don't like the idea of your father around you, my dear, so I just had to tell you it was me she saw. Don't let her drive me out of your thoughts.

I obviously had told Norman I had seen the gypsy lady, so I then told him what I had heard from Freddie. That night I sat and asked Freddie if he was glad I had told Norman about what he had said to me and I heard a very loud "NO". This took me completely by surprise. But then I heard someone say, "Of course I am glad, but beware of booming voices from the spirit world because others can interfere." I am adding this because it taught me a short, sharp lesson that not everything that comes through from the spirit world is nice.

Chapter 15

To me this is how the first years of this experience were, just like an invisible presence. Of course it is really still just an invisible presence, but in a more intense way now.

I must include this. I was sitting meditating one evening. I can't tell you the date of this, but it was obviously after Keith brought Freddie close for me on 18 October 2002. This is what came through to me:

> *I am Ching Ling. I lived in Tibet. You would have liked me. I lived a mellow life, lighting candles, praying, being quiet. You need to let others into your mind to help you with this book. I can feel a kind of resentment from you now that I am talking to you, because you think that I am in the way of this Freddie Mercury. But he won't go away because of this. He needs our help as much as you do; this is a big task. This will not be received like the books that are written about Indian guides attaching themselves to people, although they are true; this is Freddie Mercury and the world knows the name. This will come as more of a shock to people. Open their eyes to the fact that we all live on. I myself knew of this spirit of this Freddie Mercury man; long before you, hundreds of years ago in your time. I never came back to Earth again I have always worked from here and enjoyed it. He the Mercury Man did though, to become Freddie Mercury. He I am sure will tell you this himself one day but he will not come to Earth again. He will be happy and contented now helping you write things down, having your friendship. We are all the same you know, all intermingled, and we here in*

the spirit world choose between us who will come through to you like myself. It will not spoil anything. Think of us as Freddie's associates; that maybe will make it feel a bit more intimate for you. You will know when I am around; it will sound like clinking small bells. Don't forget Tibet.

I didn't really know what this, "Don't forget Tibet" meant until very recently. My friend Joan bought a type of chime from a market. She didn't know what she was going to do with it but she walked round a corner and bumped into me and said, "Do you want this because I haven't got anywhere for it?" I thanked her and took it home. When the wind caught it I thought, that's strange that sounds like what I would imagine Tibetan bells sound like. I didn't say anything but asked Norman what he thought the sound was like. He said the same. So of course every time I hear this now I automatically think of this Ching Ling. Was it sent into my life to remind me of him? The spirit world, I have learned, sometimes attracts our attention in very odd ways.

Chapter 16

Around Christmas 2002 and into the New Year of 2003, I had a conversation with a friend about this situation with Freddie and all the things that had come through from him. He said he was fascinated with it all but he was a bit concerned just in case it wasn't Freddie.

This friend's name is Philip King. He has had some very bad times in his life, getting very low like we all do. Many years ago now when he was only a teenager he had a very similar experience to the one I have with Freddie.

He experienced someone famous who had died come close to him briefly, at a time he was feeling very down, and because of this and the fact that he didn't know what was happening it scared him. So of course he told the wrong people the medical profession about this, and he was automatically labelled as a paranoid schizophrenic because it easily explained the voices in his head. I am not saying that schizophrenia doesn't exist, I know that it does. Many years ago now I worked in a psychiatric hospital and I know what this condition can do to the sufferers, but Philip is a very good, close friend of mine so we talk freely about the voices in people's heads, my voices, his voices, and I would say on the whole we sometimes hear similar things. For example, we may hear a voice in our mind telling us something we will see later on in the day and it will come true. But I am sure that this is due to the fact that we are open to the spirit world; some people are, and some people aren't. And there is really no harm in this; lots and lots of people hear this type of thing. But of course people like Philip sometimes become very vulnerable and then they will hear something said to them that isn't so good, maybe telling them to harm themselves. But I am sure there is a possibility, in Philip's situation, that 'bad spirits' play around with his mind, because it isn't all just good stuff that is filtered through from the spirit world, and these bad spirits that have not got anything better to do prey on vulnerable people. I think somewhere along the line people have planted fairly securely in Philip's mind that these voices are demons, which I am sure they are not, but because of this Philip was a bit concerned that what I was receiving from Freddie wasn't Freddie at all, just a demon messing around with his name. So I think for a little while maybe I was a little concerned myself, because when you have conversations like this it does shake you up a bit. But I was soon put in my place, because a few days later a poem came through, so obviously everything that goes on around me is seen by the spirit world.

Friday 18 January 2003.

I just can't understand,
How you could ever think now
That this isn't me,
I just don't know how.

You've got such little faith,
About a thing such as this.
And sometimes I think,
Shall I give this a miss.

Then I think how you've helped me,
And I just can't let go.
Because I know in your heart,
That you really know.

That this isn't a game,
That it's honest and true.

This was all I got initially but then two days later the rest came through:

The days have gone by now,
And I know you can see,
That I'm not a demon,
That this is really me.

With all of your friends,
Who care very much.
And we will always stay close,
And your life we'll touch.

So please don't be worried,
The future's not bad.
It just will be different,
From the past that you've had.

It's always hard I know,
To break free.
But we can see things,
You can't possibly see.

This is your chance now,
So please give it a try.
It will all soon make sense,
And then you'll see by and by.

That your life that's in front,
Is much better for you.
But there is just one thing,
I would like you to do.

Please don't forget me,
Because I am your friend.
And I know this sounds strange,
But on your love I depend.

I've got a new life now,
And I'm happy that's true.
But what you can't see,
Is a lot's down to you.

I know you still see my days,
When I'm there at a show.
And see all of these people,
And you don't really know.

How I singled you out,
Made you special to me.
But if you look and you listen,
Perhaps then you will see.

That I was just one more person,
Standing there all alone.
Coming off that damn stage,
And thinking, who can I phone?

Who can I talk to
Tell them just how I feel?
Because I even thought then,
That that life wasn't real.

But who could you tell,
When you stood in my shoes?
Open your mouth,
And it's there in the news.

Poor old Freddie. I try not to see him as a superstar now, and it must be very difficult if you live in the full limelight and spend your life wondering if you can really trust anyone. I think this conversation with Philip was meant to be. It has certainly made me see Freddie through different eyes. I think it has probably helped Philip as well, at least I hope so. I don't think he really sees these things as demons so much now, and he is being really strong and managing to control these bad voices. He tells them to clear off a lot of the time and I think it does help. I think the main thing that pulls Philip down more than anything is that he is gay and because of this people ridicule him and his partner. If people would just leave them alone and let them get on with their lives I am sure he would be fine, but they can say what they like, I am proud to have Philip as my friend and his partner Keith, they are both lovely people. Philip has written a story of his own, a good story for other people to read. I'm sure they would find it interesting, and maybe be able to understand someone like Philip a bit more.

This is a poem, which sounds again very much like my mother talking to me. I will tell you all how it came to be written.

Norman and I live on the edge of Dartmoor. So often we go for a car ride around part of it, and it automatically brings back memories of my mum and me because over the years we often went there walking our dogs. Happy memories but tinged with sadness now, because she's gone. We were heading back home one day and I was quite choked up about my mum, and then I started hearing these words begin to come through, and also a voice in my head saying, "Hurry up and get in the house and write these words down for me while I can still hold them." So I went inside, sat quietly and listened and this is what I got. It was Sunday 16 February 2003, and if this was from my mother I am very proud of her.

I watch you worrying all the time,
But I wish you could see,
That I am really fine.
I see you crying, breaking your heart,
But now is the time,
You must make a new start.
Try to stay stronger,
I'm still by your side,
Having fun in your car,
Coming with you for a ride.
I'm still very close to you, that's why you feel such pain,
So let me try to tell you something,
I will now try to explain.

The only thing that's changed,
Is that you cannot see me there.
But I'm always there beside you,
I'm always there to care.
You were my best friend for my time on Earth,
And I'll always be yours too.
But we all want you to write this book,
There's so much that we want you to do.
You were always wanting to help someone,
To give them strength, a chance to carry on,
A shoulder to cry on, someone to listen and to care.
Wanting to help the lonely people,
Letting them know that you were there.
Well by writing this book that's what you will do.
Send it out round the world,
Let them learn something new.
Give them new hope a new chance to see,
What it's like for us here, how we are already free,
And together and spurring you on.
Because we are all glad we've known you,
Glad you're the one.
Who can spread this good news,
About Freddie and his gang,
Help them listen to his voice,
And the songs that he sang?
Tell them listen to the words,
How he tried to tell a story.
Help us stand him in the light,
Let them see his glory.

Chapter 17

Sunday 8 June 2003, my birthday.

Norman and I met my girls for lunch and then we had a walk around a car boot sale. On one of the stalls someone was selling Elvis memorabilia. My daughter likes Elvis so we stopped and browsed. The stallholder said to me, "Wouldn't you like an Elvis calendar?" I replied that I liked Elvis but it was Freddie Mercury I was interested in. This man retorted, "Oh Freddie Mercury was all right if you could just hear his voice but you didn't have to look at him." So I instantly saw red, but kept very calm. My family all took a step away from me because they thought I was going to erupt, but instead I just calmly said, "Well I can assure you there are a lot of people who really miss Freddie." He said he was sure there were but he didn't like him because he was gay. So I asked this man what that had to do with anything, Freddie was an entertainer and what he did in his personal life was his own business. People say my eyes flash when I get angry and I think this man saw this, so he tried to mellow it down a bit and said, "Well, there is a group in Exeter called Mercury and they are so good that Freddie Mercury's family came to see them. Maybe you would enjoy seeing them." So I very proudly said, "Oh yes, that was Peter Freestone, Freddie's personal assistant for many years, he came with me to see them, I know him very well." This certainly shut the man up, he didn't know what to say. Good old Freddie, I thought, he's done it again, because I know he led me into this situation. It's like he is walking beside me sometimes.

And while we are on the subject of gay people, if some of us were a bit more open minded and tried to understand these people or just accept them, it would be even better. Because we don't know what may have happened to them in their young lives that makes some of them live this way. Look what happened to my friend Mike, his life was ruined. He didn't want to be gay; he got married when he was eighteen and the marriage lasted only a year, because of his previous history. And he was still talking about his wife right up until the last time I saw him, desperately upset even then that he couldn't have stayed married to her. How do we know certain things didn't happen to Freddie in his young life at these boarding schools he went to? I'm not saying anything did, but how do we know? From what I have heard, he never talked about his childhood. Why? We all talk about our childhood at sometime to someone.

There was an attitude that we all had to adopt when we became volunteers at the AIDS centre, that was to become non-judgemental, and my way of thinking is that we should all try to live this way. All you need to do is get to know a person and often you will find that a completely different story unfolds about that person. There is so much more we could do to help one another, and the world if it comes to that, if we weren't so quick to judge.

I will just add one more observation: if something did happen to Freddie when he was young, who could he ever tell? Like he said in his poem, "Open your mouth and you're there in the news."

I did find a Queen song very sad, its called 'Mother Love'.

What was he crying out for in this song? I'll let you all make your own minds up on this one. Here is another poem I received on 3 June. I have started timing them now and I would say they take on average seven to ten minutes. I am including this one because there seems to be some anger in it. I have had a few come through that seem to include some sort of anger on Freddie's behalf. So I thought maybe it is best to let you all see this side of him too.

Turning and spinning,
Swirling and whirling,
Free as two birds,
That's how we are.
Holding on tight,
Because the flame is now burning,

Like a bright star,
When it glows in the night.
And others will see,
That it's happened to them.
A friendship like ours,
Is like one perfect gem.
How can you compare it,
With things you can buy?
So just open your hearts,
And reach for the sky.
Let this love in,
Don't push it away.
It's there for us all,
Can be found every day.
So let's start a new way,
Of us living.
Don't take pleasure from taking,
Try giving.
That's what we must do,
Respect one another.
Treat all of the world,
Like they are your sister or brother.
Help where you can.
That's one thing I must say.
Lean towards others,
Who need your help every day.
Try not to be selfish,
Giving yourself so much wealth,
Learn from my life,
My friends
Don't hoard it all up,
Until your life on Earth ends,
And then having to watch from the other side,
These people having a joy ride.

On 8 June 2003 my daughter Rachel bought me a book for my birthday called *If the Spirit Moves You*. It's about a lady whose sister has died, and really her search for her, wondering where she is, eventually going to spiritual people and mediums to see if they can reach her sister for her. All my daughters know that I am interested in anything spiritual, not just Freddie. But because Freddie has come into my life I had every intention of reading this book. I read the first few pages, found it interesting and then put it to one side until I had some free time, because at that time my priority was getting the book written. On Wednesday 11 June a sudden overpowering panic hit me that someone else had written something in a book about Freddie linking up with them spiritually, to the extent that I phoned Keith and told him this. He told me not to worry about it and just keep writing. But on Friday13 June my daughter Paula phoned me and asked if I had read the book Rachel had bought? I said no, but I would get round to it. Paula told me she had bought a copy for herself and had almost finished reading it and she couldn't believe what she had read because it mentioned a lady in America, a medium, who was sometimes in touch with Freddie, and really she felt the same way that I have done over the years, partly afraid that the wrong people get to hear. I was shocked at first and maybe a bit upset in case someone beat me to it in publishing a book like this, because it isn't an easy thing to write about and takes a lot of time and dedication; it is very important to me and has become a big part of my life and always will be. But then I thought, no, this is good really because it will make my book easier to believe if other people have had spiritual experiences were Freddie is concerned. Maybe we can even back each other up eventually and then that will make it even more obvious that we all will still exist on the other side of our earthly death.

I am sure the book that Rachel gave to me for my birthday was guided to me to let me see this small story about Freddie in it; and I'm sure I was meant to meet the rude man on the car boot sale and be able to put him right on a few things. I am convinced that Freddie guides me into these situations to help make the book more interesting.

I received the next poem on Saturday 14 July 2003. There is a certain amount of anger in this one too. I believe from different experiences I have witnessed and things I have heard that people do carry some hurts and a certain amount of anger about situations for a long time after their earthly death, and I also feel that if people can't make themselves say a personal sorry to these people on the other side the anger and hurt don't subside. This also obviously follows on from what my daughter told me she had read in the book.

This is the proof that you need my dear,
Finding out others feel me around too.
Then it helps to convince the people you see,
That what you are saying is true.
This isn't a joke and it isn't a jest,
But there's a long way to go yet,
To convince all the rest.
So the more that come forward,
And say yes this is me,
The easier it will be for others to see,
That the story that you're telling
Is just full of love and hope,
And the relief I'm sure it will bring.
But finding out I still exist,
Won't go down good in few places,
And I'm sorry to say,
But I can't wait to see,
Those bloody people's faces.
I'm sorry my anger is all sent to you,
But releasing it makes me feel better.
It's a shame we can't publish all of this dear,
It would be better than sending a letter.
But I'll just say thank you for caring
And listening.
So let's relax now and see,
What this book's going to bring.

When people read this book I am sure Freddie will be really excited. He won't be bothered, I don't think, about people who don't believe all this, but I know he will be very happy about the ones who do. And I am glad I can do this for him and all you people. So take from it what you can, even if you can't accept that this is Freddie Mercury. It may open something up inside you, make you think differently about life. I am sure there are a lot of people out there who have felt Freddie's presence somehow. I would be pleased to hear from you.

Chapter 18

I have actually got to the stage now that I don't see anything strange any more about the communication between Freddie Mercury and myself, I just accept it all and treasure it, and think of him as one of my best friends. I will try to explain another aspect of Freddie being around me, which has nothing to do with writing this book, just closeness and friendship I would say.

Norman has to take about six tablets each morning and he always puts all of them in his mouth together. I said to him more than once, one day you will choke on those and there won't be anyone around. But Norman is a bit on the stubborn side and doesn't really like to be told what to do. So I thought the best thing I could do was not worry about it.

A few mornings later Norman was getting his tablets sorted when I distinctly heard a sing-songy voice sing words from a Queen song called '*Another one Bites the Dust*'. I remember thinking, Oh that's strange why has a bit of that song popped into my head. I had no sooner had these thoughts when I saw Norman choking really badly on his tablets. It's lucky I was there. I told him what I had heard said to me. Ever since that day Norman has taken his tablets separately. Norman and I are convinced that Freddie had been watching this situation and thought, well, he won't listen to Mary so I will make him see the danger. Another strange thing is that Norman has been taking these tablets for about ten years and has never choked before.

There is another example. We went to a place called Ottery St Mary one day. I had never been to the place before. We parked outside the church and as we pulled up I distinctly heard a voice say, "You could go into that church and light a candle for me, I like you lighting candles, it brings me closer to you." I always try to tell Norman what I hear and then if what I have heard is true that's a bonus because someone else knows. And if what I have heard doesn't happen then I still think it's good that someone else knows because it becomes some sort of a guideline to how often I hear the right thing, and I must add and I'm sure Norman will agree with this that most of the time I have heard it right.

So, going back to the church situation, I said to Norman that it couldn't be right because as far as I knew they only lit candles in Catholic churches. This was Church of England. But we went inside anyway because I do like to look around churches, and, yes, there was a place to light candles. This was at the time when I didn't know if I would be able to have my home back through my divorce settlement. So Norman and I needed to find somewhere to live after his house was sold. We found a small flat, and Norman put in an offer on it. There were other people interested too, so there was no certainty that he would get it. But one morning I heard a voice as clear as day say, "You will get your flat, go and tell Norman now." So I quickly scurried off to find Norman and told him what I had heard, and said, "Well, I've told you now so this will be the proof that I imagine half the things I hear." But I had no sooner said all this to Norman, when the phone rang. It was the estate agent to tell us the flat was ours. I cannot say that this did come from Freddie, but it certainly came from somewhere.

There have been many similar occurrences, but these were just a few examples for you. I am trying to cover all the difference aspects of my communications with Freddie. So here is a different story again.

On Friday 18 April 2003, Good Friday, I drove out to Buckfast Abbey to light a candle for my mum, Jake, everyone that had either passed over or was in despair that I knew of really. But I always light an extra candle just for Freddie. Ever since he told me, through Keith, that he likes me lighting candles for him. But when I got to the Abbey I discovered you could not light candles on Good Friday. It is regarded as disrespectful to Jesus because he died that day. I can't understand this reasoning because I thought he was supposed to represent eternal life. So I went back home and lit my candles there. I sat down in front of these candles and said, "What a day, Fred. Have you been watching all that, and can you see that I have finally lit a candle for you and I do think of you all of the time?" This is what I received, not instantly, but later in the day.

Words are so inadequate,
Our feelings to convey.
When the heart is full,
We often find it hard to say.
How much we appreciate,
What other people do.
But I hope these lines express,
My gratitude to you.
For your friendship,
For your help,
And for your sympathy.
You will never ever know,
How much you've done for me.
When I needed someone you were there,
To help me through.
So these simple words of thanks,
I'd like to send to you.
Brief they are,
But truly meant.
And with warm affection sent.

As I have been putting this book together I am obviously drawn to anything with a spiritual interest and I have noticed that there seems to be more programmes on television about this type of thing, especially on Kilroy. I try to watch them calmly but always get agitated because some of the people are trying to tell a story, or maybe convey a message they have had, or a spiritual experience, and there is always someone really rude that has no intention of listening; they for some reason try to shout these people down. I realize we have all got our own opinions, but I am sure there is no need to be so rude. Are these people half afraid of this type of thing, and is that why they make a big hoo-ha about it all?

I was watching one of these programmes on the 16 June, and there was a girl trying to tell a story about her mother when she was nineteen, who had a conversation with a gypsy lady who told the girl's mother that she would have four children, three girls and one boy, but she also told her she would be dead by the age of forty. I must add my own comment on this. I don't believe it is right to tell anyone such information even if they have got the ability to see these things. But this girl's mother was indeed dead by forty. There was some man shouting this poor girl down saying it was rubbish. Well, now I will tell you a story of my own, and then you can all decide for yourselves if it is rubbish.

Three months before my grandson Jake fell into the canal a man, a psychic artist, came to a town close to where I live. I went to see him with one of my daughters and her boyfriend at the time. We had decided to go because my daughter's boyfriend's brother had died at the age of nineteen and her boyfriend was obviously devastated. So I persuaded him to come along, hoping we could get some news to give him comfort. The idea was to give a photograph of the deceased person to this man. Some messages did come through for my daughter's boyfriend from his dead brother, and am sure it did ease his grief a bit. But then the man looked at me and said, I have got something here for you. I had no photographs with me, but he still brought this through for me.

He started to draw a nun, and underneath, he drew a little boy. He said that the nun from the spirit world was trying to protect a little boy on Earth. He was between three and four so watch out for something that might happen. By the side of this little boy's face he drew a small picture of the cartoon character Tweetie Pie. He said he didn't know what any of this meant but just to watch out, and, to be honest with you all, I didn't think any more of it.

I kept this drawing but didn't really even look properly at it. Three months later, Jake fell into the canal on the day after his fourth birthday. I remember thinking, as we were on our way up to Bristol, my God that's what that psychic artist must have been talking about. How did he pick up on that? Three months after Jake's accident, this psychic artist returned to our local town. So I went to see him and told him my story, but there was not an ounce of sympathy in this man. He just said, "Oh, that was just a premonition I picked up on. Our lives are mapped out." And he walked away from me.

When Jake eventually left the hospital and went to live in the respite centre, someone had attached a Tweetie Pie balloon to the handle of Jake's buggy. Rachel and I followed the ambulance in my car and all the way this Tweetie Pie balloon tapped against the back window of the ambulance.

So are our lives mapped out for us? I have still got the drawing that this man did; it is in all frame at the top of our stairs. Another remarkable observation is that the little boy's hair in the picture has been coloured in red; Jake has very prominent deep auburn hair. I keep this picture where I can see it every day in the hope that, if it was conveyed from the spirit world that this terrible event was going to happen to Jake but they couldn't prevent it, they will surely take care of him when the day comes that he will have to leave us.

But of course there is another side to all this. When you are forewarned of such a tragedy, after it has happened, you remain full of guilt with thoughts like: why didn't I warn my daughter of this? Why didn't I make sure Jake was better protected? But how can you? What can you do? My daughter has told me many times that if I had told her what the psychic artist had told me she wouldn't have taken any notice of it because she would have thought it was all rubbish.

Chapter 19

I have had many vivid dreams about Freddie Mercury, memorable dreams not just whimsical ones, and I will tell you about one of them.

But first I must share with you a very vivid dream I had about Princess Diana, because I feel it would be very unfair if I didn't include it. I have never had any more since, no more experiences at all where she is concerned except for what I told you earlier in the book. This is the dream:

It was about ten days after Jake had his accident, which makes it 30 October 1997. So as you can see Diana had died only a couple of months earlier. In the dream I was walking down a long corridor, which was fairly brightly lit. There was no one in this corridor except me and I was walking along quite happily I would say. And then I saw a lady walking towards me and, as she got closer, I realized it was Princess Diana. She came straight towards me, and reached out her arms to me and I remember saying, "Oh Princess Diana it's you. What are you doing here?" She said to me, "Don't call me Princess, just call me Diana, or else they won't let me stay with you and I need to stay with you for a while because something is happening concerning you." She gave me a long hug and then she just seemed to be there with me for a long time, and then she was gone.

I woke up with a start and looked at the clock; it was 3.15 am. I fell back to sleep and I don't think I would have thought much about it the next day. I would have probably just put it down to the fact that she had got lodged into my memory because I had been in London for days after her death. But the next morning at about 10 o'clock Jake's mum phoned me to tell me that Jake had had a heart attack just before 3 am. So is Diana still helping from the other side? And had she somehow seen the situation that Jake was in at the time, and had just chosen to be with me for a while in my dream. I think there is a very strong possibility.

If anyone else has had dreams of Diana I would be very interested to hear from you.

It seems to me there are two types of dreams: one of them seems to be just muddled up events, and flashes of memories of these dreams but nothing you can hold on to; the other type is something very, very vivid, something you don't forget as the years go by. I had a vivid dream concerning Freddie, which I will never forget, but I will just tell you a short story first. For a few years I was very good friends with a husband and wife who were foster parents. They basically fostered special needs children; they adopted two of them, and were a very close, happy, fun to be with family, and I loved to spend time with them, but they had had some sadness as well. The girl of seventeen who I mentioned earlier in the book died suddenly was their foster daughter. They were also emergency foster parents. So one day, out of the blue (strangely enough the very same day that I told Peter my story about Freddie) the social services turned up on this couple's doorstep with two small children, a boy and a girl. It was supposed to be a temporary arrangement until they could be placed somewhere more permanent, but time went on and these children were still with this couple. So of course my friends started to get attached to them. A while went by and then I had a very vivid dream in which I was in this couple's house. I came out of their kitchen into the hallway and Freddie Mercury was standing there as plain as day. I remember saying, "My God, Freddie, I can see you so clearly, what are you doing here?" He approached me and said, "To show you something." He wrapped his arms tightly around me and swirled and swirled me along the couple's hallway and into their front room, but by the time we reached the front room it wasn't Freddie in my arms it was the little boy that the couple were fostering. I put the boy down on the settee. Freddie was still there, somehow. that's the only way I can describe it, as I couldn't see him. He was saying, "Promise me you will never stop visiting this couple, promise me, promise me", and then the dream was over. I phoned my friends the next day and told them about my dream, and I said to them, "You will keep these children, I know you will." Their answer was, "No we won't, they will eventually be taken to younger foster parents and anyway the Social Services would never agree to us keeping them because of our age." To cut a long story short, they did keep the children and have since adopted them. But because of this situation, sadly they had to move out of the area. I did continue to see them, so Freddie got his promise fulfilled, but it was because I wanted to see them not to please Freddie.

It was actually at their leaving party that I met Norman, so is that what Freddie was leading me towards? I have never seen this couple since that night, but we do occasionally keep in touch, so I am sure we will get together again one day. I do hope so.

I will tell you one more of my vivid dreams, which I will never forget. Not long after my friend, Mike, died I dreamt that I was walking down a leafy lane, and someone caught up with me and linked their arm in mine. It was Mike. I don't remember being shocked to see him, and we walked together for a while but neither of us spoke. Eventually we came to a caravan, just ordinary, nothing fancy. But it was more like a residential caravan. He opened the door and followed me in, it was still nothing fancy, nice I would say, but not special. And then Mike said to me, "Open the other door and step outside." I opened the door and there was a beautiful stream running by, with lots and lots of rocks in it, making it more like a waterfall. I have always loved the thought of living by water. Also, at the back of the caravan, was a completely private area where you could be completely alone if you wanted to. I said to Mike, "This is lovely but what's it for?" He replied, "It's for you, for your future. You can go there whenever you like and be content." And then it all just faded away. I must have carried on sleeping, and I just woke up naturally the next morning, but the dream was really vivid in my mind. This dream I would say took place sometime in 1998, so not recently.

My friend Joan, who is typing this book out for me, lives on a residential caravan site about a mile away from us but this site is set more in the countryside. There are also holiday caravans there. I had had this idea for a while that it would be quite nice to buy a cheap holiday caravan and maybe rent it out to people;

just a small interest in life really, something to do. Norman and I had been asking around different places, with no luck. And then one day we asked Joan whether there were any holiday caravans on her site for sale. She said she would enquire for us, and it turned out that there was one for sale, not very expensive at all, and it was tucked away at the very back of the site. She told us that we couldn't rent it out but our family would be able to stay in it, so it might be worth a look. So I went to see this caravan and I would say as you approach it from the front it looks fairly ordinary, but when we reached it and went round the other side of it there was a beautiful babbling brook and a private area at the back surrounded by woods. I instantly fell in love with it and just had to have it, and in no time I had bought it. It has turned into my personal little sanctuary. I bought it at the end of April 2003 and this is where I have sat and written this book. I already had the bulk of the information written down, here and there, but this is where I have put it all together. Who would ever have thought all those years ago that I would be sitting in a caravan somewhere writing a story about Freddie Mercury? But Mike must have known even then.

While I am on the subject of Mike knowing these things from the spirit world, I will tell you all part of a reading I had with a lovely lady who is a very popular medium, and obviously very good at linking in with the spirit world. This reading was done for me on 18 January 2003. This is how it started:

> *There is a gentleman here wanting to connect up with you. He died in his middle forties. In the end he died of a chest condition. He is showing himself young and strong, how he liked to look. This gentleman is calling you, my girl; he is saying you looked after him. He is saying everything was wrong with him by the time he passed away. He is saying to me, tell her this was such a special friendship we had. I know I became very emotional with you, but you always listened. He says, I don't think most people saw the depth of our friendship. He is saying you gave him youth again and he is saying you had lots of conversations about the spirit world. Things he needed to*

know. You gave him lots of this information. He is saying I know I argued with her about these things but she gave me my strength back. He is saying there were other people in my life but I didn't really have a lot, but she was always there, close, giving me strength and she gave me special cards and words of hope through the post sometimes. He is saying tell her thank you so much. He is saying she brought the light back into my life. He says you have got a photograph of him when he was ill, and he is saying, my God, don't I look a mess, I don't like that photograph, tell her to throw it away. He says you should see me now. He says you dreamt of him and he's saying, yes, it was me. I also walk with her all the time. She's aware sometimes that I am there and whenever things get bad she usually talks to me. And I do talk to him. He is saying she never let me fall; I'm not going to let her fall now. He is saying she touched many souls, she has a gift. I know now that I am able to see it all, she has the spirit world working with her all the time.

This is just part of the reading. This medium lady didn't know anything about my life, so it was sent through to me from the spirit world. So I hope it helps you to see, if you can find a good, true medium, how much information you can have sent through to you from someone you miss, and it proves that we do live on after death, or else where does all this information come from?

Chapter 20

I have been told off by the spirit world about certain things I haven't mentioned in this story of Freddie. Obviously they must be important so I will include three little stories.

I explained to you all in Chapter 2 about meeting Bruce James and going to his home sometimes. Apart from being a medium, he and his wife also run a small animal sanctuary. They had a friend in London who worked in a laboratory, where they bred cats. I won't go into all the details here but there were two cats that needed a home, and for some reason this lady brought these cats all the way to Devon to Bruce's house hoping he could find homes for them. I gave one of them a home. She is a tabby and white cat; she was seventeen months old at the time and I called her Emily. Time went on and Jim Hutton wrote a book about himself and Freddie. In the book are pictures of Freddie's cats and one of them looks just like Emily. So I showed Emily this picture for some reason, and I remember saying, "Look, Emily, you look just like one of Freddie's cats." As I said it, it felt to me as though someone was leaning over my left shoulder. Although there wasn't anything to see I really could feel this presence, and whoever it was was possibly saying something to Emily. But what convinced me that it was not my imagination was that I realized Emily was staring wild eyed at my left shoulder. She shot under the table and sat there staring at something for ages. So she must have seen something, and they do say animals can see the spirit world more easily than we can.

Then there was the day that it was in all the newspapers that Ayrton Senna, the racing driver, had died; it was 1 May 1994 I was reading these stories and remember thinking what a shame, but it didn't have any deep emotional effect on me. And again I felt a very strong presence around me, something leaning again over my left shoulder, like someone might stand and look over your shoulder and read the paper with you. But of course there was nothing to see, just this strong feeling. And I heard someone say, in my mind not out loud, "If you don't believe that this is me, Freddie, around you why aren't you crying about him? You didn't know of him any more than you did me. So your emotions towards me should help you believe all this."

My third story happened in 1999 when I went to the Queen Convention. The reason that I went was because Peter was living in Torquay at the time and he ran a coach from his hotel. My friends said it would do me good, take my mind off worrying about Jake, just for a few days. My friend Vivien said she would share a chalet with me, so off we went. It was in Prestatyn, North Wales so it took a long time to get there, but we had Queen videos playing on the coach all of the way. There were people on the coach who had travelled over from America and other countries to stay at Peter's hotel and then go to the convention. So I must say I did feel out of my depth because, remember, I wasn't a Queen fan as such, although by now I did enjoy their music and songs and loved anything concerning Freddie. While we were at the convention I must say I found it enjoyable. One evening there was a tribute to Queen and somehow I got separated from my companions and ended up in the middle of a crowd of people on the dance floor. They were all really enjoying themselves, singing along and calling, "We love you Freddie", and I can remember now the feeling I had. It was just a very overpowering feeling of, this is never Freddie Mercury that comes around me, how can it possibly be? He was such a star and so well loved, he would never bother to reach out to me in this way. And I remember feeling very sad about the fact that I must have been wrong all along. Of course, prior to this I had already had masses of evidence that it had got to be Freddie around me, but this experience of seeing all these people just swept it all away. I did enjoy the rest of the convention but afterwards I felt I had lost something special and I think sometimes even if you are aware of the spirit world you can easily shut it out and I think I closed it out for a while. Looking back now I realize, to me it was better than having to face the fact that I must have imagined all these things about Freddie.

Time passed and life just went along as usual. But the spirit world must be stronger minded than me and see things in a completely different way, because in November 1999 I decided I would go to a Spiritualist Church, just for a change really, and I received a message that really threw me. The medium said:

> *I have got a gentleman here for you dear, he says he used to be an entertainer, a singer. He is saying you know who he is anyway, and he is saying, where have you been I have been waiting for ages to talk to you to tell you that I am really glad that you went up to North Wales earlier in the year and had a good time. I was watching you and saw your sadness about me. You must know by now that this is me and I won't leave you.*

The convention had taken place in May 1999, so quite some time had passed by and this message certainly made me feel better. It was unexpected and overwhelming but it encouraged me to start mixing again with more spiritually minded people. Of course there is another way of looking at this: for all you Queen fans if you were there in 1999, Freddie saw all of you as well!

Chapter 21

On Monday 14 July 2003 I went to a small meeting in the town where I live, to try to learn how to read tea leaves. I thought, well this will certainly be different. I was sure I wouldn't have a clue how to read them, but as the evening progressed everything was explained to us. We all paired off with someone we didn't know and the idea was to have a go at reading each other's teacups. It was just for fun really, just a happy, social, chatty gathering. The lady I was paired with and I started chatting, looking into each other's cups and reading from a chart to determine what the tealeaves we were looking at might mean. She asked me, "What does Freddie Mercury mean to you?" Well I certainly couldn't understand how she could possibly see anything to do with Freddie in a cup. So I tried to keep my face as calm as possible and asked her, "How can you see that?" She replied, "Because he is standing by the side of you, I can see him clearly. He isn't like a spirit, he looks real. He is wearing a dark green slightly shiny suit." She was absolutely shocked, I know she was, and so was I but I couldn't see anything. Then she said he had gone, but that he was just standing there looking at me.

So I told her I was writing a book about him, but asked her not to tell anyone because I didn't want it to be known who this person was until the book was finished. She promised she wouldn't, and I asked her if she had ever seen him before in that way, and she said, "No, never. I have never seen anything like that before, only my family in dreams." I can assure all of you this certainly made us lose our concentration on the tea leaves. I really don't know how Freddie managed to do that, but of course this gives more proof that he is still around and I get the feeling that as time has gone on he is enjoying his new life. I'm not so sure about his earlier experiences of passing into spirit but I am sure he is happy now and is enjoying all this.

I must say that I was very proud to be able to tell this lady that Freddie had been around me at certain times ever since he passed to the spirit world. But I was quite surprised that he could be bothered to come to a place like that with me. I'm sure he planned it because I wasn't going to go to this meeting but I changed my mind at the very last minute. It was the same with this lady who saw Freddie; she too had only decided to go along on at the very last minute. I personally think that what Freddie is doing is trying to get more and more people to see that he still exists. I don't know what the dark green suit represents, maybe nothing, but again maybe someone will recognize something in this when they read about it.

One night during the time of writing this book, Norman and I went over to my friend Keith's house for a social evening, just a chat and some supper. Of course we did talk about Freddie and what else he might tell us, but we didn't try to connect up with him at all that night. We were saying we wondered if it was possible for Freddie maybe to be able to tell me what it was really like in the spirit world, how all these spirits live their day-to-day lives, shall we say, because I must admit I had often wondered about this.

I must add this before I go on: I can't just bring Freddie close to me on command; if he doesn't feel like conversing with me he doesn't. I just don't want you all to get the impression that I chat away to him every day, because I don't.

A few days after we had spent the evening with Keith, I did sit quietly and say, "Come on Freddie please talk to me and try to explain to us all what it's really like in this spirit world. How do people live their lives there?" I heard this come through to me:

> *As much as I would like to tell you, dear, there is a universal law that doesn't allow me to. The reason for this is that if people living their earthly lives knew this information it would be too tempting for some of them and they might try to shorten their lives on Earth and that isn't the way things work. I can tell you this, that if*

you live a good life on Earth you will instantly reap in all your rewards when you come back to the spirit world and you will all carry on growing in knowledge and be able to become whatever you want to become part of in the spirit world.

He said the most important information he could give me to pass on to you all is that "There is no death"; that this is the main reason for this book: to make people understand that our lives do go on after our earthly death; that we instantly become free from any pain we might have had to suffer on Earth; that we will see again everybody that we loved while we were on Earth. He said he knows his name will carry a lot of weight and that will, he hopes, make people take this in all the more. He said he wants his friends who think they have felt him around them to know for sure that it is him and not their imagination. He wants people to care for each other more, people in all walks of life. He said from where he is now he can see that this is the only way that this world of ours can improve and become a better place. He also wants us all to understand that when we leave this Earth and go to spirit we instantly know what is happening among the people we have left behind. We can see if they are not carrying out our wishes, breaking promises. So please all of you, don't say things that you don't mean to these dying people just because you think that person will be dead soon so it doesn't matter.

He did say he could tell you that anyone who has had a near death experience, or has died for a short while and then woken up, shall we say, whatever they saw that was good, they should hold on to that and share it because they have found part of the truth. He said he is sorry that he can't tell us anymore but even he has to abide by the laws.

Chapter 22

I have done a lot of thinking about the next story I am going to tell you shall I include it in the book, shall I not? But I have decided that I must do so; if I didn't I believe it would be very unfair of me. I will tell it to you in exactly the same way that it happened to me, or came to me shall we say?

On 24 June 2003 it was a lovely sunny day, so I decided to sit in my garden for a while and meditate, more with the idea of just drifting off to sleep, I think, not expecting at all that I would pick up on anything. But after a while I could hear the song 'More Than a Woman' running through my mind. So I sat quietly thinking to myself, that's a Bee Gees song, who's this around me? And I heard as clear as day in my mind, "Maurice Gibb." So I replied, "It can't be Maurice Gibb. You can't get through as easy as that." But I heard in reply, "Why not? Freddie does. It's him who taught me. Can you tell everybody that I am all right, I'm safe and happy. Can you just put a couple of lines in your book please? That's all I want. Can you tell my family that I do miss them all but not as much as I know they miss me, because I spend a lot of my time around them. "Hearing all this came as a real shock to me, because I have got used to Freddie coming through and have accepted it but this was a complete surprise. But the next day, 25 June, this poem came through:

If I have a little chat with you today,
Will it make any difference to the way?
You think of this thing about Maurice Gibb.
Or do you think it's rubbish,
And we are telling you something glib?
Because it isn't like that at all my dear.

This thing you heard is completely sincere.
He just wants the people to know that he's free,
And his life carried on in the same way as me.
I know that we ask you a lot of hard things,
But it gives you a chance,
And it takes away the sting
From the people who have lost us,
Or that's what they think.
So what's the point of worrying,
If you cause a bit of a stink?
And I know what you're thinking,
That I am safe where I am, using you and abusing you,
As though I couldn't give a damn.
But you're so wrong you know,
You're just precious
And you just haven't a clue,
What you are doing for us.
I will bring great comfort you know,
Because it's so hard for our close ones,
When we have to go.
But to find out we are still living
It's a wonderful way of giving
The best gift in the world,
There could ever be.
So surely we could do this,
You and me.
Don't be afraid my dear,
Just tell them that now, this man is here.
You don't have to make a fuss,
Or tell a long story.
He isn't looking out for some great glory.
He is just hoping and humble in a way.
So I told him I would persuade you.
I would say,
Come on my dearest friend,
Please try and help us,
Just do it simply.
No need for a fuss,

Let's give him a gift
Between you and me
Just let's help all his family,
Show them that he's as free as me.

One of the reasons I have included this is that the day before Maurice Gibb died I had completely made up my mind that I was going to rip the contents of this book up and just put it out of my mind forever. But then when I heard of his death all I could think was, my God, it's bad enough when anybody dies but when it's a star like this it completely rocks the world, and this is when I decided I must carry on writing this book. So you could say Maurice Gibb was its saving grace.

But also I have included it because I have twin daughters and strange things happen between them, for instance they experience each other's symptoms, just like Robin Gibb explained in a newspaper article, saying that he felt nauseous at the same time his brother was in hospital with pains in his stomach. But Robin must try to understand that he couldn't have saved his brother's life just because he felt this happen. I do understand what he is going through though, to a certain degree, because there is something about twins that binds them together. And I know for sure if anything fatal happened to one of my girls the other would be lost for the rest of her life. And another reason I have included this story is because Robin Gibb also explained about his brother's brain damage, and it's a similar situation really with my grandson Jake. Lack of oxygen to the brain created the brain damage, but unfortunately it didn't destroy the brain stem with Jake and this is what has trapped him his present situation. His life, I can assure you, has no quality at all, but the poor boy can't even release himself from it. So only through this experience in my family am I able to say this: if anyone has been faced with this situation in their life because of a loved one, please be glad that they could die with some dignity and please try to draw strength from the fact that we do all live on.

I hope the Gibb family are able to read this and I do sincerely hope it gives them some sort of comfort and helps them to accept the fact Maurice is close to them. Why shouldn't he be when Freddie Mercury can get so close to me?

Chapter 23

Now it would be a good idea to return to Freddie with the following story.

On Monday 21 July 2003, Norman and I, together with and my friend Joan went to see Keith with the intention of his, hopefully, bringing Freddie through for us. Joan came along with us because of her fascination with this story now, but also as a witness, in a way, that this is all true.

For a while we just sat and talked together, sharing our own personal thoughts about the spirit world. We all more or less agreed that there must only be part of the whole of whatever we really are in a spiritual sense that comes down to Earth to live the earthly experience. I am telling you this because later in the evening when Keith went into a trance for us it came out that the spirit world, or Freddie, was listening to our conversation.

So this is what came through while Keith was in trance. Keith's spirit guide came through in the same way as on other occasions, just to greet us and say welcome, and preparing the way for the Mercury Man to speak. He said:

> *There is no such thing as peace and quiet on your Earth anymore and this makes it more difficult for us to come through but we come because we care about what is going on in your world. I have sat with two of you people before and the third person, the lady Joan is very welcome. The man's mind, Norman, is more open now to the idea of the spirit world. All of you enjoy your searching for the truths, enjoy your enquiring minds. The Mercury Man will speak to you now.*

This is what he said:

> *Mary, Mary hello again. I'm always coming close to you, Mary. I'm always coming to impress my mind on yours. You pick my thoughts up really well, you don't know it but you do. You must be beginning to know that it's not your own mind or your own thoughts that are coming through to you, that you write down. They are mine. You've done well with the book. This book will now soon finish but you must leave it open to carry on into another. As you carry on writing it will be about time. When I was on the Earth plane time was of the essence. Everything that I did, every song that was written was about timing. Did you know there was a Mary in my life when I was on Earth? I have a very strong memory of a Mary with me. If you keep continuing the way you are going it will be nothing but success what you write about me. You are searching for answers on how to finish this book. Just write it like it is, that's all you need to do. Every thought that comes into your head about me add to the book. This is a book of my life, but it is a book of my life which has continued since I physically died. When you are looking for your words to come together, try as often as you can to forget now Mercury the singer. Say things that come into your mind that you receive out of my mind. Write down what you are instructed to write and nothing can go wrong. Of all the things to write about you have chosen the hardest thing to write about. About me, Freddie Mercury, because this isn't actually about me the man this is about me from the spirit world, about me returning to converse with you. Tell the story of the spirit that you believe in as well, Mary. Of what you yourself know to be the truth of the spirit world. You will find as the times goes by you will become more and more spiritually aware. The more you allow our minds to mingle with yours the more you will become aware. I am much more than Freddie Mercury now; I always have been, I just didn't know it. We lose that memory while we are living on Earth. I was*

listening to your conversation earlier expressing what you yourselves thought of the spirit world. This is how it is, just part of us comes to Earth, like a fragment of the whole thing, but when we leave this Earth it all falls into place again. So sometime in the future write down your own thoughts, Mary, on these matters. I will help you all the time, I will be there, how shall we say, almost hovering over you. You see you have a mind that I can work through easily. People will maybe say, well she's certainly got a wonderful imagination, but if you didn't have an imagination for me to work through how could you possibly imagine that a man supposedly from beyond the grave could come through you and transcribe words to you and express what he wishes to say to you. You are all seeing a change in the world. In my world, the one that I left behind, probably more than in your world now, there is, I can see, a change of attitudes. If the change of attitudes had been there before when I was a young man, before I was, and I use the word very loosely, a celebrity, I think I would have been a different person. I never felt I was exactly who I really was, I had to lead that flamboyant life, I had to live the life that people expected of me, but it was a façade it was not the real me. Those who knew me, who knew me well, saw that there was a much deeper person underneath all that, but I never seemed to get a chance to express it in public. One of the reasons that I have been working through your mind, Mary, and still am, is to try to express what I wanted to express when I was young. I was a student with very high ideals, revolutionary thoughts. Just because you die or you have been famous or because your life changes in one way or another doesn't make you any different inside; I have still got these ideas in my being. You now live in a world that is changing very dramatically in every way but there is more tolerance in the world that was not there when I was a young man on Earth. I have lived other lives in addition to this last time I was on Earth, I lived in Aristotle's time, but this is all for the future for you to tell this story; it's too much for you to absorb at this time. I must go now. The medium, my friend, is tired, so I will say so long, we will talk again soon.

I must say that I found some of the things that came through this time quite disturbing. I find it hard to let go of Freddie Mercury himself and try to see him as something different, because it has taken me years to accept truly that this is Freddie with me. So for a while it left me feeling very disoriented about all of this and not quite sure how to carry on with the story. But I did hear Freddie say to me as we were leaving Keith's flat that night, "Can you tell Keith for me that it would be better if he did a straightforward reading for you, instead of this trance thing. I feel completely controlled coming through to you this way and I am quite capable of coming through to you myself now. You will see all this worry of yours differently if I could just talk to you more directly."

I did mention to Keith what I had heard Freddie say but he had got another busy spell in front of him, being away from home a lot, so we had to leave it for a while. But Keith did agree to do this for me as soon as he had some free time. However, two days later the following poem came through and it did make me feel a bit better.

Wednesday 23 July 2003.

You mustn't lose hold,
Of this thought of me dear.
Your friend Freddie Mercury
Will always stay near.
It's just that things change,
In the same way over here,
As if I'd stayed down on Earth,
So let me try to make things clear.
Look at your own life,
How it's completely changed around.
Writing this book for me,
The new person that you've found.
So now your life is on a different track,

And I hope it brings you joy my dear.
There are many things it could bring.
It could open up a new life for you,
Help you meet all kinds of people,
Open up a new world for you,
Give you a chance for all your dreams
To fulfil.

So this is what's happened to me you see,
Things have completely changed around.
I can't stay Freddie Mercury For eternity
That was just a part of a time that I found.
But that doesn't mean that you'll lose me.
I am also part of your time.
And all of those memories
Are locked there inside you.
No one can touch, they are yours and they are mine.
I will always treasure
The time that you spent,
Writing this book for me.
And I'll always remember
This time with love.
Drawing closely together but you'll see,
As time goes on it will all make sense,
And I know the response to this
Will really be immense.
And before you know it you will be writing again
And all of this sadness will pass.

And I'll tell you things
About how I live now.
How our life changes to a different way.
To freedom, to peace and I just need to say,
Just hold on tight,
Don't ever let go,
And I'll stay close beside you
Telling you all you need to know.
And it will all be so exciting

You finding out such things,
And all of the people getting to know,
And all the joy it should bring.

I must say that this poem coming through to me did ease my mind a bit about all this. It seems to me when I look at this complete story that every time I got myself in a muddle about how to put it all together to make sense to you all a poem would come through and to me they all contain a kind of a story of their own.

Chapter 24

For a while I couldn't seem to concentrate on how to finish this book, being disoriented about this situation with Freddie, trying to accept him as someone, or something else now. But also I was going through a spell of worrying about my grandson Jake. It had been suggested that he should be fostered out. The leaflets were all sent out to prospective foster parents in a ten mile radius of Exeter. My daughter Rachel was absolutely tortured by this because her access to Jake would be limited as it would for the rest of the family, and also a lot of money was being offered to these people to take on this responsibility, so we were afraid of the situation as well. But up until now no one has come forward and hopefully they won't; Jake needs special nursing care. As things calmed down a bit about Jake and I tried to open my mind to this Freddie situation again, the following poem came through. It was on Wednesday 13 August 2003.

We are all revolving,
All around you,
You just can't see us there.
Like a big wheel
On a fairground
And everyone of us care.
We are trying to open up your mind,
To catch what we are wanting to say.
There are so many things,
That we all want to tell you.
We try to make you aware,
Every day.
So listen a bit harder,
My dear, my friend.
You've already been told
This story has no end.
Now it isn't just me

Who's talking to you,
Everyone's trying to chip in.
So we will have to work out something
So that you know it's me,
Or else how are we going to win?
It's you and I that started this story,
Now they all want to have a go.
So I'll try to speak harder,
Than the rest of them.
That will be the way that you know,
That it's me that's talking to you.
So just go along with the flow If you can.

A few days after this poem came through a voice or a thought in my head said, "Keith is at home today, phone him quick before he goes out." So I made the phone call expecting him still to be away, because he works at Belgrave Square Spiritualist Association for about eight days each month, but low and behold he answered the phone. I told him what I had heard and that this was why I had phoned, and yes he should really have been away from home but he had had to cancel because of illness. So this just proves how the spirit world can see us so easily. I made the phone call because I trust what I hear more now. At one time I would have just ignored this voice and would have thought it was my imagination.

Through this phone call we made arrangements for myself and my daughter to visit Keith on 19 August, but at the last minute my daughter cancelled so I ended up visiting Keith on my own. And I believe that this is what Freddie was hoping for. Knowing him the way I do now I expect he arranged for it to work out that way. So below is my reading from Keith. I am more or less including the complete reading so that you can see that all of these people can get through to us quite easily once they have learned how to, but I am also lucky having Keith Hall as a friend because he is a very good medium.

My mother was the first one to say something, and if you take note of it all you will see that the things she brings through are more stunted than those that Freddie brings through. I would say, and this is my opinion, that the longer you have been in the spirit world the clearer the messages you are able to give. Anyway here is the reading, so see what you think.

My mum came through. She was talking about her stuff, her furniture. She was saying about November being an anniversary. It could be my gran she was referring to, as she died in November, or she could have been talking about Freddie passing away in November. She told Keith she had heard me talking about her furniture very recently (I had been talking about a particular chest of drawers of hers the previous day) and then she said that all the sisters each had had some of her stuff when she died (my three daughters were all given some of my mum's things). She was telling Keith about a special stool that I had got that belonged to the family (I have got one of my gran's old stools which had been in the family for years). Keith said he had been aware of my mother's presence with him ever since he had opened his eyes that morning. She told Keith to tell me that she was sorry for the way she had behaved in the last few months of her life (she was very awkward with me and very hard to please). But in my eyes it's just old age that can bring that on and she shouldn't feel she has to say sorry for that. She was my mum and I loved her. And anyway if anyone should say sorry I should be saying it to her, because it really upset her when I left my husband. She said to Keith, "Tell Mary I died so peacefully, it was a beautiful passing over to where I am now." She said she was ready to go, she was tired of her old body and all she can remember is that she fell asleep and when she woke up her mum was there waiting for her. Keith said to me, "Your mum is here now looking at you saying, don't worry about me it was all wonderful when I arrived here, I had time to say my goodbyes to you all before I died so it all worked out right." I don't remember her saying goodbye to me, but as my girls left the hospital the night before she died they all kissed her in turn and she said to them, "You are saying your goodbyes to me."

I must add a personal note. It was so comforting for me to hear all this, because we were all expecting a very uncomfortable death for my mum because it was discovered that she had an aneurysm about a year before she died. Since Freddie has come into my life

I have learned a great deal about spiritual matters, about different energies that we can call on to help people through bad situations, and I believe this is what helped my mum to have this easy death. We all do these things in different ways but how I tried to help my mum is each night I would call upon what I called 'my mums angels' and I would ask them if they would stay round her bed and let her sleep well, because for a long time she had had an inoperable hernia which caused her great pain and kept her from sleeping, but often she would phone me in the morning and say, "I had a really good night's sleep last night with no pain at all." I never told her about these angels because I was afraid it would worry her. I must stress, however, that you do have to ask for this help, it won't just automatically happen. The day that my mother was taken into hospital I knew she wasn't going to live, so there was only one thing that I could do for her, as I saw it, and that was to call upon mum's angels and ask them to take her back home peacefully, and it seems there's a chance that it worked.

There were a lot of things said to Keith that day that was sent through to him from my grandson Jake's little mind. As I have told you before, whatever Jake's mind is he can communicate with Keith, but because of his mum's feelings and also the fact that it is very hard to take on board that a child like Jake can communicate this way, I won't go into this now, but who knows one day I might write a book about Jake. But I will tell you this much. Jake tells Keith that when he is asleep he is free from that body and travels into the spirit world and spends time with people (spirits) there and this bit is important so I will share it with you. Jake told Keith that he knows Michael in the spirit world, and then Keith said he could hear someone calling out, "Tell Mary this is Michael here now." This was unarguably Mike who I made friends with through the AIDS centre, because whenever he comes through to anybody he always says, "Tell her it's Michael." He said:

> *Tell Mary I know about Jake's mind being free as well, he often tells me things... Can you tell Mary thank you for being there for me. I've cried on her shoulder many*

> *a time...Mary used to fill all my forms in for me I did for any hospital appointments and other things...I am glad my life is over, tell Mary that can you, that all the spiritual things I used to talk to him about he had found out to be true when he arrived in the spirit world and he said it really helped him when he passed over.*

Mike also said:

> *Tell Mary I still remember the Scottish man we knew. If you ever meet him again can you say thank you for being there we did know a Scottish man at the AIDS centre who was a volunteer, and he often talked and listened to Mike...People talk about going to hell but you will find out when you get to this side you can live your hell through your earthly life. I went through hell when I was on Earth but I have found my heaven now...explain to Mary that we don't go to hell when we die not any of us. We used to talk about these things and worry about them but the hell we worried about I have discovered is what we suffer on Earth not here. Not after death of the Earth takes place... Tell Mary I did some bad things in my lifetime, she knows anyway because I talked to her about most things but just remind her will you and tell her I was paid back for that over and over again through my illness...Tell her I know she has a photograph of me and she still treasures it and that makes me happy.*

All these things that Mike said to Keith make sense and are true. He told me many more personal things as well that are all true. There is no doubt at all in my mind that this was Mike talking to us.

There were a few messages for me from other people and everything that was said was true but I don't really think it would be of much interest to all of you so I have now skipped to the part that I am sure you will be interested in.

Keith said:

> *I have got Freddie Mercury here with us, as clear as you can get anybody through. He is looking very pleased with himself and has got a big smile on his face. He is saying, "I have been waiting eagerly to speak to you; I have been waiting patiently while the others spoke. I was, shall we call it, overseeing the rest of them. It's almost as if Freddie is part of your crew" For a long time I have been calling Freddie the leader of the gang. He is saying "Tell Mary we have got a real intimacy built up between us now." He is really smiling about this and saying we have got an intimacy of the mind. He is saying "We have built up this real closeness. You will get a certain amount of ridicule about this book but I just want you to know that I had that all my life, Mary, but you are strong enough to take it and I will stay close by you. There is one person that ridicules her now and it really hurts her." There is one person who does this and it does really hurt so Freddie is right and it proves he can see this but I am not willing to say who it is. But he is saying, "Tell Mary not to worry about it everything will turn out all right. I sent something to her recently to prove to her how close I was to her. Tell her the silver star she saw was me in the room with her.*

I was absolutely shaken when I heard this because a few days earlier Norman came downstairs with no shirt on and he sat down on a chair. I noticed firstly two very small shiny dots on his back. I actually thought it was some sort of glitter on his back but when I went to brush them off they absorbed slowly into his body. Neither of us could understand this at all. Then Norman walked into the kitchen and I noticed a slightly bigger, silver, shiny, star like shape on his shoulder so I told Norman to stay very still and I would have a good look to see what these things were. This silver star like shape stayed there longer than the others, about a minute I would say, and then that one absorbed into Norman's body too. We were completely bewildered by this but this is obviously what Freddie is talking about. Has anyone else ever experienced anything like this?

Freddie also said, "I removed a book out of Mary's house but now she has found it again" I did lose a book that I was reading. I searched and searched everywhere for it and it had simply vanished. It was called Hiding from the Light and it is all about witchcraft, and then I went to a car boot sale and there was a copy of this book on a stall and by it was a book called *I* Stole Freddie Mercury's Birthday Cake, so I bought both of them. The book that I bought turned out to contain only two pages in the entire book about Freddie. So obviously this person had just used Freddie's name to promote his book, which did at least prove to me how much weight Freddie's name carries. But how a spirit can remove a book from your home I don't know. Maybe it was annoying him because I was spending to much time reading that and not writing for him.

Freddie then said, "What goes on around this woman is amazing. If she could just learn to trust in me a bit more and accept all this. If she would open her mind to me a hundred per cent she could learn all sorts of things." He said if I could just trust and accept him things would go really well. He said he is quite happy himself with the way things are going, that I receive what he is saying in a natural way which is exactly what he wants. He said, "Tell her everything is going to plan." Then Keith said:

Freddie is saying something really strange now. I feel embarrassed to repeat it but he is saying tell her about the cornflakes; I was there when she was looking at the cornflakes."

This obviously sounded like nothing to Keith but to me it was amazing. The day before this reading I was in a supermarket and there were some cornflakes on offer: two packets for the price of one. As you all know I am writing, this book in a caravan I bought. But preparing food is a nuisance when you are trying to concentrate on writing so I was thinking that these cornflakes would be ideal for me to eat while I was writing; just pour some milk on them and it's sorted. I didn't actually buy them in the end but the amazing thing is Freddie obviously knew about this situation so these spirits must go to all sorts of places with us.

Keith even said, "Well, that's amazing. I almost didn't tell you because it sounded so silly. But Freddie is laughing now. Then Keith said does Freddie ever swear at you because he is swearing while he is talking to me." (So now that it has come out like this I will tell you, yes he is capable of swearing at me, which I wouldn't have mentioned, but of course it does make him more real and easy to accept.)

And then Freddie said, "Put this in your book: I'm a spirit not a bloody saint! I haven't suddenly become holier than thou just because I exist here now." He also said to mention that I had a mole on my face. (I don't know why this is important but maybe someone will understand the meaning of this.)

And then Freddie said, "Mary squints a lot, you know. Her eyesight isn't that bright these days. I watch her especially at night and she is looking for something. I think she is looking for me."

Actually all this is true. My eyesight isn't so wonderful anymore and I do sometimes squint, as Freddie calls it, around the room at night. Because sometimes I do see shadows in the room and try to catch what they are, more than anything because our cat, Emily, and our other cat, Sidney, both sit and stare in the direction of these shadows and they say animals can see spirits. So it is again proof that he draws really close to me. Both Keith and I did have a really good laugh about this situation and apparently Freddie was laughing as well, saying it's so funny watching Mary because she is actually seeing we spirits but she can never quite catch on to what they are. He said, "Tell her I have got an advantage over her; I don't need eyes to see where I am now."

Freddie continued:

> *Tell Mary I love this intimacy of minds that I have found with you. It's really nice to have found a mind that I can be comfortable with and it gives me so much joy...I had a host of friends on Earth but nobody really knew me. Mary seems to know me and that's what I like. Even now people are still searching to find out what Freddie Mercury was really like. Do you know why they are still searching for so many things about me? It's because nobody really knew*

who I was. They all thought I was the party man, they saw me as the gay man. It seems to me, looking back, that's all the people in general thought I was...Once when I was writing a song someone said there was like an aura around me. Someone will remember this. Even when I was on Earth I was aware of the spirit that was within me and even with that knowledge that was within me I still didn't do anything about it, I had to die to do something about it. I knew there was a spirit world. I knew about the auric field that worked within me when I was writing. I knew my inspiration was coming from a spiritual source. I don't mean the way that Keith does it. I don't mean that; I didn't understand all that then. I'm on about the creative spirituality that was within me. But I have come to realize that all this is one and the same thing. As soon as I arrived here in the spirit world I knew that it was all one and the same and I almost instantly knew that I hadn't finished with my life on Earth completely. I just knew there was something else that I had to do concerning Earth and this is it. Proving to you all that we don't just die. I did make a comment on the Earth plane once to someone, that if there is a life after death I'd want to come back somehow. Someone will remember this comment. Does someone remember?

Freddie says that he does hope that I will get confirmation of this. (I hope so too.) I find it all so intriguing. Then Freddie said:

Mary will get a little bit of controversy about this and she will think, I'm going to stop all this. I don't think I want to go on with all this. She's already had these feelings many times and thought I don't know maybe I'll just keep all this for myself. She won't she won't keep it to herself, because she is finding out her own truth on all this. As I know this truth in my heart she knows it... Tell her about Katie, I really have not got a clue what this means, but I think it's best mentioned. Maybe it means something to someone else?

Keith said, "I don't know anything at all about Freddie Mercury but I am quite surprised at the sound of his voice, it's quite a deep voice, a very well educated voice. Does that sound about right to you, Mary?" To me that was spot on because I have always thought since taking so much interest in him that he spoke in a way that I would consider quite posh.

Freddie then said, "I knew what I was doing. There was never a time when I didn't know what I was getting up to and that I didn't know I would have to reap the consequences of. I was never stupid and I was never unaware of where my life was going to lead to an early death. I've always known it." Keith said by making this comment Freddie must have carried a premonition of an early death. (But, strange as it is, I must add that I do remember reading somewhere that Princess Diana felt this as well, that she wouldn't grow old. I find it very sad that some people carry this through their lives.)

Then Keith asked me, "When you where young did you have an invisible friend? I feel that you had quite a lonely childhood." (I did have quite a lonely childhood and I do, funnily enough, remember inventing as I thought at the time invisible friends, but now I am wondering if they really were with me.) He continued, "I think you have got an affinity with black people, can you understand that? Black people or spirits shall we say in your young life. It seems like you have got an affinity with black people from many, many years ago and it upsets you that people were so cruel to them." (I must say that if I watch films where the black people are being treated badly it really cuts into me to see it. Especially a film that I watched called *Beloved*. I watched it really because it was about a spirit still around of a child, but the cruelty to the black people in that film was like torture to me. When other people watch these films they just seem to say, "That was a good film", and I usually end up arguing with them saying, "Don't you care how these people were treated?" But I think everyone else thinks I'm mad.)

Then Keith said, "It's funny but I can see this black lady with you, its almost like she has known you for always. She is almost like a guardian angel with you. She is saying when Mary was a little girl she had a golliwog that she loved (this is true.) She is saying, I know all about the story of her golliwog."

So now I had better share the story with you all. When I was a very little girl, one of my mum's friends made me a golly. She stuffed it with sawdust, a strange thing to do I know, but this is all part of the story. I really loved this golly and took it everywhere with me. But one night it got left out in the rain and, of course, all the sawdust got wet through and my mother had to throw it away. I remember crying for days about this, so it seems this black lady spirit must be around me if she knows about that. I myself had forgotten all about it years ago.

Keith said, "I have got a feeling there is an affinity with this black momma and Freddie. Did he like black music?" I don't know much about this but I have heard that Freddie was inspired by Jimi Hendrix but I am not sure if this is the black music that Freddie is on about. Then Keith asked, "Did Freddie ever go to New Orleans?" (Again I don't know.) He continued, "I think Freddie is saying that he had some sort of spiritual experience around that area."

This is when you will all have to bear with me because this is all new to me as well remember, just because I have accepted that this is Freddie Mercury in my life certainly doesn't mean I can understand everything he tells me. But I am including it, just in case someone else understands, because as far as I am concerned this book is for everyone who reads it. It's written to learn from, gain some kind of comfort from, for many reasons, and if you decide you don't like what it contains then the best thing to do is to throw it away and forget it.

Keith said, "What Freddie is trying to confirm to you is an answer to something you have always had in your mind ever since he came into your life really and what he is trying to tell you without worrying you too much is, yes, you have known each other in other lifetimes. But he knows you don't really like anything concerning reincarnation and he doesn't want to scare you off."

I must admit it does make more sense of all this but, no, I don't really like anything to do with reincarnation. It isn't really my past lives that worry me it's the thought of having to live another life down on this Earth that bothers me. Because my hope is that when my life is over, and hopefully not yet, I will stay in the spirit world and help somehow from that side. But, yes, it does make more sense if I have lived another life knowing

Freddie or whoever his spirit was then, or else how did he find me so easily? Keith then said:

> *Freddie is saying, one of our times together was in a black existence in the black areas of New Orleans. Music is part of my soul. Freddie is saying we did know each other well in that existence and please add this in your book because this is the beginning of another story. Tell Mary to sit and meditate quietly and see what she receives from me. She will at first think, this is my imagination, but tell her let it happen. If I, Freddie, didn't have these thoughts and this imagination how could I ever have imagined that one day I could come through to you from the spirit world like this? How could I ever have imagined that I could be such a famous singer and entertainer. Tell Mary not to worry about it, to just go with my flow and see what happens. She's come this far and been this brave. This is all for the future for her to write about so tell her just to listen to me and let it happen.*

Then Keith said:

> *Freddie comes over to me as a mischievous person and he is saying this will shock them all. He said: I loved shocking people, I always did. If I was at a party or something like that I would say the most outrageous things just to shock people but that wasn't the real me, but it gave them something to write about. Not many people knew who I really was and I liked to keep them guessing. It's only since I have been back in the spirit world that I have learned of these other lives with you, Mary, I didn't instantly know as soon as I arrived here, it took time, but I have known for many years in your time now. But I thought it was best kept from you until you had almost completed this*

book or else it all would have been too much for you to take in. If Mary could just link in a bit deeper with me I will now start to tell her about these lives. We first started off in the seventeen hundreds when the slave trade was rife. Try to imagine this life we lived and then you will start to understand better why you get upset when you watch these things. (And then Freddie mentioned Bristol was important that made no sense at all to me but my friend Joan told me that they used to bring the slaves to Bristol all those years ago. So maybe that's what he is trying to say.) Mary is always asking me questions, you know, wanting to know this, wanting to know that. Well here is an answer to one of her questions. I know that she had always worried that I have maybe been alone here but I had a father figure in the spirit world that helped me when I arrived.

Then Keith asked, "Did Freddie have two people that he looked upon as dads in his life?" I couldn't answer this except I remember reading that when Freddie was young he spent a great deal of his school holidays with relatives, so could it be something to do with that? Freddie continued:

So the answer to Mary's question is, no, I have never been alone here. And many of us musicians gather together here. We are drawn to likeminded people in the spirit world. So tell her not to worry I have never been alone here. There was a list of people in the spirit world that I had known on Earth also, so I spend time with them. Tell the people who remember this that I spend time with Paul. Tell Mary I am very aware of little Jake's spirit with me often. He said tell Mary that what happened to her Jake, it was all meant to be, it's all mapped out for us like a pattern. If Mary always sees things in black and white she will never understand this. Tell her to try to see beyond this situation. Tell her to try and open her mind up to much vaster things than just life spent on Earth, because everything that happens to people on Earth is almost like an illusion. The spirit within us is the true us, and these Earthly lives are just part of eternity. She has already accepted, because of you Keith, that Jake can still communicate and I just want to tell Mary that her grandson is more alive and living that anyone could truly understand. The drama of these things that come into people's lives has to be to make other people learn in their lives. Even the terrible situation in Ethiopia is for a reason, to help people learn and help others and I only know this now because I am back in the spirit world and am able to see it all. I wouldn't have understood any of this when I lived on Earth. I have always wondered this and I often used to say years ago, I think I have landed on the wrong planet. I seem to sometimes be an odd one out here. Mary has never really and truly been at peace with herself. She is just beginning to find that peace now. I know who Mary truly is, I've always known. I didn't know her in my last life on Earth but now I am spirit I realize I have always known Mary.

Keith said, "He's laughing now because some people are going to think, who'd have thought it would be a bloody woman because people will mostly remember him as having a man in his life." But then Freddie said, "I did have a woman in my last life as Freddie Mercury. I loved her from the very depth of me." He went on to say that I had really loved him, Freddie, in another life, that's why I am so drawn to him now. So Keith asked him if we were married in this other life, but he said, no, it was closer than that, we were more like brother and sister. Freddie then said:

This reincarnation, they have all got it wrong, it's not really what people think, it's only part of us our spirit that comes to Earth. The main part of us, the real spirit of us stays here. Mary's head is always full of questions, but that's good. I like that because if she doesn't ask questions she won't get the answers.

Keith asked, "Do you find Freddie impolite sometimes as though you ask a question and he just replies 'Oh just get on with it.'?" This is true. Sometimes I say, "For God's sake Freddie, how am I going to tell the people that?" and he'll say, "Oh just bloody do it!"

We then asked Freddie about this song he keeps on about me trying to pick up on and this is what Freddie told us:

> *Write it about the children, put in this song 'Today Tomorrow and Forever.' (Keith said that sounded like a title) Try to write this song in a spiritual nature. I was always aware when I was writing my songs that there was something around me, helping me. I didn't understand at the time what it really was but you do, Mary, so try to use it. It wasn't until I died that I realized that we all have that spirit within us all the time we are on Earth. All I have done by coming back to the spirit world is to swap minds I am the same person I was on Earth but this part of me that is talking to you now the only way I can explain it to you all is the spirit within. Let me come close to you in the same way that Keith does and I'll tell you this song. Imagine I am in the room with you, try to visualize me there. That will help because it will build up the closeness between us and then you will hear me better. Light candles also; I love candles, they draw me closer, and I need you to discipline yourself a bit more, Mary. Pick a time of the day that you will give to me, to listen to me, and I will be able to tell you all you need to know. You need to attune yourself to my energy. Let us greet each other and spend on hour each day together and the rest of the day just live your Earthly life. Let's try it like that. Because you are panicking about finishing this book you are not listening properly. Try to listen the way you used to listen when I told you all these things earlier in the book. Of course I realize you were more relaxed then because you never really thought this book would come together and now you see it will your mind is all over the place and I can understand*

that. This is a big thing you have taken on but because I was a professional in my career, in my singing, I think maybe sometimes I expect too much from you. I would have quite liked writing myself to be honest with you. I did start to put a book together about myself, but it was never completed. I don't know if anyone knows about this book that Freddie started to write but this is twice that he has told Keith this now. Keith, when Mary was young she liked to sit and write stories, that's why she has been able to put this book together so well. I know everything about Mary's life from the minute she was born into your world, but of course only since I have been back in the spirit world. This is where all things fell into place and made sense again about our previous lives and the people we shared them with. This is how I know Mary so well now and this is how I know about her since she was born this time.

There was more said to Keith and myself from Freddie about how all his previous lives were involved in music in some way, about how music is part of his very soul, but it is all very complicated and I need to digest it all before I start trying to explain it, so I think that's best left for another time.

Freddie then said to Keith, "Tell Mary goodnight. Everything's doing fine, don't worry." Neither Keith nor I could understand why Freddie would finish off with goodnight, but I must admit it did give me a warm feeling because I sometimes through these years have thought I have heard someone say, as I was falling asleep, "Goodnight, sleep tight." Maybe that was Freddie all along, so I think this is an ideal time to close down the communication from Freddie in this book. I am sure there will be plenty more in the future.

I do hope that some of these communications I have received make sense to some of you, and if any of you feel that you have felt Freddie's presence around you please let me know. I would be very interested. I am sure I am not the only one.

Chapter 25

With regard to this song Freddie has mentioned at times, I have tried to put one together and here it is. As you all will see I'll never be a famous songwriter.

September 5 2003 (Freddie's Birthday).

There are flowers in your garden,
There are birds among your trees.
But there are children out there crying,
Saying, can't you help us please.
I haven't got any food to eat,
And nobody seems to care,
Will somebody help us, and sing us a song,
Someone famous, who's living out there.
Today, tomorrow and forever,
We need to send out this big plea.
Please send a message around the world,
Open their eyes, make people see,
That if you don't stand up and fight for us
Then our small lives were all in vain
And the road that we walk in despair
With no hope
Will happen again and again.
But if people gathered together,
And formed some sort of a crowd.
And were all very strong,
And delivered this message real loud.
All that we need is some love,
And some care.

And some thoughts of kindness,
From all of you people out there.
I'm a little boy called Jake,
So use my name please for everybody's sake.
I'll be an example to let people see,
That there's so many kids around,
That need love and care Like me.
There are children who are starving,
Children who can't walk.
Children out there like myself, my friends,
Who cannot even talk.
So can you give us some dignity please
Somebody famous out there.
Spread this message around the world
Ask the people to listen and care.
So you people with your flowers in your gardens,
And your birds among the trees.
If someone will sing us a song,
To you all,
Can't you help us somehow please?
And then,
Today, tomorrow and forever,
Perhaps the world will improve.
And we will never
Have to ask again,
For your help in this way.
And if this song helps
I myself Jake will say,
Thank you my friends for caring
And finding it in your hearts
To be more sharing.

So there it is, that's the best I can do, and I don't want any of you people thinking that I am trying to make my grandson any more special than any other child in any sort of trouble. He isn't, they are all important but sometimes if people who can don't step forward and help such people then their lives are all in vain. I've only used Jake's name as an example because I am on the side of seeing these things.

People have always told me that I put everybody else before myself. So just this once I am going to say, if I could had one wish for myself it would be for Robbie Williams to sing a song on the lines of the one I have tried to put together and I would like to set up some sort of a Trust for children in distress. I am sure Freddie likes Robbie Williams, I am sure he sees in him partly what he would have liked to have been himself. Robbie Williams doesn't seem to have any problems at all regarding relating to a crowd. Whereas, even though everybody loved Freddie, by watching videos of him I would say that he was always a little bit reserved and maybe that's some of what Freddie partly meant when he mentioned earlier on in this book that people are more tolerant of things these days and he was sure he would have been a different man if people had been more tolerant in his day. But besides all this I think Robbie Williams must like Freddie or Queen in general because I watched his show from Knebworth House on the television and I noticed he included the song 'We Will Rock You' in his show. So come on Robbie Williams, would you like to do this for us, for the memory of Freddie? It would be very much appreciated. It might even give me a chance to meet you and give you a hug, just for being you and the happiness you create among the people who enjoy your songs. In my eyes you are very special. All through writing this book I have often had Robbie's album *Escapology* playing in the background. It seemed to make it write easier to write for some reason.

The reason I was drawn to this album was because my daughter Rachel had it playing one day when I visited her. I remember saying to Rachel, these words sound like my situation with the book I am trying to write. So she lent the album to me and I'm afraid I've only just returned it to her. I found I liked all of it so you could say Robbie Williams is absorbed into this book anyway.

Chapter 26

I would just like to mention Peter Freestone again briefly. I have often sat and wondered about this situation with Peter. We had got to the stage, or at least I had, when we had decided to be friends without Freddie in the friendship. That sounds cruel, I know, but I felt that even though we would never have met if it wasn't for Freddie, being friends with Peter was now a separate thing. But then it seemed that as fast as Peter had appeared into my life he had gone out of it again. I must add that this was mostly my fault because parting from my husband left me very disoriented for a while. Anyway, I sometimes still ponder on how all this happened with Peter, but one day I heard Freddie say very distinctly, "I couldn't have that dear, I wasn't expecting you and Peter to become friends. How were you going to write this book for me if you were close to Peter? No one would have believed you. But I would be very happy if you two met up again now that the book is written." So, as I have suspected all along, Freddie can be a bit of a control freak. But I suppose he is right; if I had become really good friends with Peter I couldn't have written this book.

So Peter, wherever you are, thank you for coming into my life and I'm sorry you've gone back out of it again. Maybe we will meet again one day; that would be nice. With Mr Mercury around it seems anything's possible. Be happy with your life.

I would like to say a big thank you to my friend Keith Hall for helping me to get the communication, through from Freddie on all these occasions. Without his friendship and his sincere help this book, I am sure, would not have had any deep substance. Maybe I would have written it anyway, but it has given me much more pleasure receiving so much communication and now things seem to be making much more sense to me as the book has progressed. Finding out I have lived in other lifetimes with Freddie Mercury's spirit helps to clarify why all this has come into my life. Now reincarnation doesn't seem so bad at all.

I would also like to thank my friend Joan for typing all this out for me. As I scribbled away and handed it all over to her she is the one who put the story into chapters. I never thought of anything like that, I just kept writing, so also without her help I think this book would have been a bit chaotic. So well done Joan, you've done a good job.

Also thank you to all my friends who have supported me at different times through Jake's traumas. I may not see some of you now but I haven't forgotten you.

There are just a couple of other points I would like to mention. I remember reading somewhere that when it was announced, shortly before Freddie died, that he had AIDS he commented on the fact that now the world will know. So I am saying this on Freddie's behalf that now the world will know this, that Freddie Mercury didn't die. He lives on in another way, whatever that way may be, and can still reach us if only we will listen. Also, because of my interest in Freddie Mercury over these years, most people that I know think that it's because I was a fan so they tell me if there is anything going on locally concerning Queen, tribute bands, someone impersonating Freddie, and sometimes I go to see these people and I can honestly say, as the years have gone by, that people seem to love Freddie Mercury more, not less. You hear them chanting "We Love You Freddie" so I'll shout out with them "I Love You Freddie".

This has been no bed of roses,
No pleasure cruise,
I consider this a challenge before all human race.
But I ain't gonna lose.
Because We are the Champions
My Friends.

God bless you all.

Also Available

Guided by the Light

Described by Professor Hans Holzer, a leading authority in America on the paranormal, as the greatest medium of our time, Philip Solomon shares his amazing story, from his childhood psychic experiences of been born into a mediumistically gifted family with show business connections, through his many strands of spiritual and psychical development, to the finely honed, highly attuned state of awareness he has achieved. For those of you who think that mediumship is merely passing on messages from beyond the grave to members of a Spiritualist church or theatre audience, then your eyes are about to be opened, as this book covers predictions, meditation, hypnotism, sports psychology, guides and angels, ghosts and the paranormal, healing, astrology, leylines and UFOs, with an emphasis on the innate ability in each and every one of us to develop psychic awareness. With a fitting foreword by respected fellow-medium, Derek Acorah, this book will definitely challenge your perceptions and broaden your outlook on life, both on the earth plane and in the spirit world beyond. In this and his many previous books, Philip Solomon's intentions and convictions are clear. He has been chosen by Spirit to walk a sometimes difficult pathway on a mission to prove beyond doubt the existence of life after death and other-worldliness and to assure those that have lost loved ones that death is not the end.

Heavens Fire

Three thousand years ago one of the earliest scriptures ever recorded, the Book of Enoch, Noah's great-grandfather, was written; 365 of the scriptures contained therein had been discovered, but one was missing. This lost parchment was purported to provide startling details of encounters with benevolent alien beings called The Watchers – information that could challenge and change traditional perceptions of mankind and the world. Oxford University professor of theology and languages, Donald Bryan, finds himself propelled from his university safe haven into the world of espionage, greed and corruption, accompanied on his roller-coaster adventure by National Security Agency agent Fae Winters, in a puzzle-solving, heart-stopping race against time to find the lost scripture before its secrets fall into the hands of fanatical religious groups. Everything you think you know about the world and its history, including the true identity of Christ and the secret inner workings of the US Government and influential worldwide corporations, will be thrust into doubt. Heavens Fire raises a crucial question: is there any truth? And the shocking answer is: those who know don't care; and those who care don't know.

Lightning Source UK Ltd.
Milton Keynes UK
UKHW011218160919
349872UK00001B/94/P

9 780993 337123